Your
Horoscope
2022

....

Virgo

24 August – 23 September

igloobooks

igloobooks

Published in 2021
First published in the UK by Igloo Books Ltd
An imprint of Igloo Books Ltd
Cottage Farm, NN6 0BJ, UK
Owned by Bonnier Books
Sveavägen 56, Stockholm, Sweden
www.igloobooks.com

0721 001
2 4 6 8 10 9 7 5 3 1
ISBN 978-1-80022-530-5

Written by Belinda Campbell and Denise Evans

Designed by Simon Parker
Edited by Suzanne Fossey

Printed and manufactured in China

CONTENTS
. . . .

INTRODUCTION
· · · · · · · · · · · · · · · · ·

This 15-month guide has been designed and written to give
a concise and accessible insight into both the nature of your
star sign and the year ahead. Divided into two main sections,
the first section of this guide will give you an overview of your
character in order to help you understand how you think,
perceive the world and interact with others and – perhaps just
as importantly – why. You'll soon see that your zodiac sign
is not just affected by a few stars in the sky, but by planets,
elements and a whole host of other factors, too.

The second section of this guide is made up of daily forecasts.
Use these to increase your awareness of what might appear on
your horizon so that you're better equipped to deal with the
days ahead. While this should never be used to dictate your
life, it can be useful to see how your energies might be affected
or influenced, which, in turn, can help you prepare for what
life might throw your way.

By the end of these 15 months, these two sections should
have given you a deeper understanding and awareness of
yourself and, in turn, the world around you. There are never
any definite certainties, but with an open mind you will find
guidance for what might be, and learn to take more control of
your own destiny.

THE CHARACTER OF THE VIRGIN

· · · · · · · · · · · · · · · · · · ·

As kind as they are critical, as down to earth as they are successful, Virgoans are the perfectionists of the zodiac. They set ideals for everyone, themselves included, to strive towards. Ruled by Mercury, the planet of communication, they will happily offer their opinions on any given subject, both when asked to and when not. Whilst communicating is a forte for many Virgoans, their sharp tongues and analytical brains can mean that their opinions sometimes come across as being overly critical. Extremely detail-orientated, and with the highest of standards, others can seem to fall short by comparison. However, any criticism Virgoans offer will usually be constructive and full of good intentions.

In opposition to neighbouring Leo, the sign of Virgo belongs to the sixth house, which focuses on health and service. Others often look to Virgoans for help and guidance about dieting or big decisions because they know that they will receive practical, informative and candid advice. Virgoans may well be nicknamed 'Dr Phil' (also a Virgoan!) in their group of friends. As well as giving second-to-none counsel, Virgoans are efficient, resourceful and have exceptional attention to detail. Such strong attributes can help Virgoans to become the highest of achievers, but their humility means they are unlikely to let any success go to their heads. Virgoan superstar Beyoncé, for example, is known for her humble attitude despite her incredible accomplishments and global fame. Symbolised by the Virgin, modest and sometimes shy Virgoans will remain as well presented and orderly as their daily to-do lists. They do not usually opt for anything too showy, as is their more introverted, negative way. Born at the end of summer when the leaves begin to transform in colour, Virgoans are a unique combination of certainty, control and change, which allows them to be both organised and organic.

THE VIRGIN

Not to be taken too literally, the symbolic sign of the Virgin represents many qualities in good, yet sometimes naïve, Virgoans. Astraea, the Greek goddess of justice and innocence, makes up the Virgo constellation and is often depicted as the Virgin symbol. However many compliments Virgoans may receive, they will likely remain modest and could come across as shy, giving them an air of innocence that can be highly attractive. This purity can be why they are often seen as being very prim and proper to the outside world, but their qualities are measured best by their ability to always find the good. Virgoans tend to be fair and true thanks to their methodical ability to weigh up the facts with intelligence and honesty, much like Librans. Demeter, the Greek goddess of harvesting, is another deity associated with the Virgin symbol. Holding a sheaf of wheat, Demeter is the mother of Earth's fertility and the reason we have seasons, which is perhaps why mutable Virgoans – with their foresight and love of planning – can make wonderful agriculturists.

MERCURY

The speed at which some analytical Virgoans process information is surely inherited from their ruling planet of Mercury, which orbits the Sun faster than any other planet in the solar system. Mercury is named after the Roman god of the same name, who is typically shown with wings on his head and feet. Virgoans are similarly quick, especially when it comes to thinking. However, the speed at which thoughts race around their heads can mean they sometimes overthink things and obsess over the smallest of details. This can make them hold a grudge better than most.

'Mercury in retrograde' is a phrase that is often met with fearful faces, but what does it mean? Three times a year, Mercury seemingly begins to move backwards and is blamed for many communication, media, technology and travel failures. Whilst many people might avoid making big decisions, signing important documents or arranging trips during a retrograde, ever-practical Virgoans will probably not let their ruling planet slow them down in any significant way.

ELEMENTS, MODES AND POLARITIES

Each sign is made up of a unique combination of three defining groups: elements, modes and polarities. Each of these defining parts can manifest themselves in good and bad ways and none should be seen as a positive or a negative – including the polarities! Just like a jigsaw puzzle, piecing these groups together can help illuminate why each sign has certain characteristics and help us find a balance.

ELEMENTS

Fire: Dynamic and adventurous, signs with fire in them can be extroverted. Others are naturally drawn to them because of the positive light they give off, as well as their high levels of energy and confidence.

Earth: Signs with the earth element are steady and driven with their ambitions. They make for a solid friend, parent or partner due to their grounded influence and nurturing nature.

Air: The invisible element that influences each of the other elements significantly, air signs will provide much-needed perspective to others with their fair thinking, verbal skills and key ideas.

Water: Warm in the shallows and sometimes freezing as ice, this mysterious element is essential to the growth of everything around it, through its emotional depth and empathy.

MODES

Cardinal: Pioneers of the calendar, cardinal signs jump-start each season and are the energetic go-getters.

Fixed: Marking the middle of the calendar, fixed signs firmly denote and value steadiness and reliability.

Mutable: As the seasons end, the mutable signs adapt and give themselves over gladly to the promise of change.

POLARITIES

Positive: Typically extroverted, positive signs take physical action and embrace outside stimulus in their life.

Negative: Usually introverted, negative signs value emotional development and experiencing life from the inside out.

VIRGO IN BRIEF

The table below shows the key attributes of Virgoans. Use it for quick reference and to understand more about this fascinating sign.

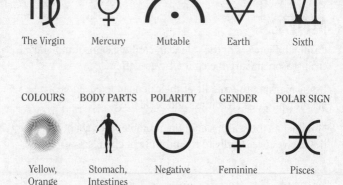

SYMBOL	RULING PLANET	MODE	ELEMENT	HOUSE
The Virgin	Mercury	Mutable	Earth	Sixth

COLOURS	BODY PARTS	POLARITY	GENDER	POLAR SIGN
Yellow, Orange	Stomach, Intestines	Negative	Feminine	Pisces

ROMANTIC RELATIONSHIPS

Virgoans can be choosy lovers. They are not often ones to frequently fall in love, but their devotion can last an eternity when finally bestowed on a worthy soul. Anyone chosen by these notoriously picky characters should feel very special indeed. Virgoans can have a tendency to find faults or nitpick about trivial matters, which can be troublesome in love. Wanting to tweak or change minor issues may seem harmless and necessary to mutable Virgoans, but celebrating the differences in their relationships will prove to be far more rewarding than finding flaws. This optimistic outlook of finding the positive needs to extend to themselves too, as they are often left confused as to what their partners see in them.

Although symbolised by the Virgin, Virgoans are not always naïve when it comes to their relationships. They present themselves impeccably to the outside world with lint rollers at the ready, but they can also be extremely laid-back when they feel at ease in a relationship. When they find themselves in the arms of true love, they will no longer worry about their hair being out of place or their clothes being creased. Curious with a mutable nature, Virgoans are often open to trying new things, which can help keep any long-term flames of love burning brightly. They may struggle initially with exposing themselves to vulnerability, resulting in them not always giving their love freely. However, when Virgoans choose to lower their emotional barriers their endless affection can be well worth the wait.

With a deeply rooted earth element, Virgoans will most appreciate partners who enjoy getting outside and who understand the importance of protecting the planet.

Eco-conscious and organised, finding someone who will go trekking in the countryside can be just as important to Virgoans as finding a partner who takes the time to separate the plastic and glass for recycling. Chores aside, they will be the most charmed by someone who brings fun and energy into their meticulously planned lives.

ARIES: COMPATIBILITY 3/5

There's not a lot that's similar about how an Arian and Virgoan think and approach their daily decisions. The Arian rushes in excitedly to almost everything, whereas the Virgoan needs to exhaust all the facts and options first. The Arian can teach the Virgoan the benefits of not getting too bogged down with decisions, and the Virgoan can teach the Arian the equal importance of noticing the smaller details in life. When these two team up, they will understand that they are very, very different, and will likely admire those differences in one another.

TAURUS: COMPATIBILITY 3/5

A Taurean and Virgoan can make for a real power couple. The Taurean's dogged approach to fulfilling goals and the Virgoan's practical and busy mind will see this pair securing a successful future together. The Virgoan can appear overly critical and may end up hurting the Bull's feelings unintentionally. Ruled by Mercury, the planet of communication, the Virgoan can be very attuned to the Taurean's needs and will try to fix any problems within the relationship. These two will likely share many things in common and can form a lifelong companionship, even if a whirlwind romance isn't in the stars.

GEMINI: COMPATIBILITY 1/5

A Virgoan may initially be attracted to a Geminian's charm and wit, but is likely to soon feel irritated by the flights of fancy. The steady Virgoan can feel too reserved for the Geminian, and the fast-paced Geminian can be too unpredictable for the Virgoan. Both ruled by Mercury and strong believers in communication, these otherwise contrasting characters may end up feeling as if they are speaking two completely different languages. However, their mutual love of change and talent for adaptability may well be what makes this relationship last longer than predicted.

CANCER: COMPATIBILITY 3/5

A practical-minded Virgoan could be the balancing force that a Cancerian needs in a partner. The Virgoan will feel loved and protected by the nurturing Cancerian, but by contrast the Cancerian can at times feel hurt by the naturally critical Virgoan. Thanks to ruling planet Mercury, the Virgoan's strong communication skills should help them patch up any problems. The earth element in Virgo and the cardinal influence in Cancer can make for a driven couple, so any loving ambitions that these two share will likely be realised together.

LEO: COMPATIBILITY 2/5

The love of a Leonian can take a Virgoan by surprise; which isn't something the introverted Virgoan is always keen on. The clear differences between the studious Virgoan and show-stopping Leonian can mean that these two might be quick to write each other off as potential partners at first glance. The relationship between this fire and earth couple can be a slow burner, but their slow and steady approach could well end up with these two winning the race hand in hand. This couple's strengths are their differences, and these two hard workers can make for a solid and complementary couple.

LIBRA: COMPATIBILITY 3/5

Both advocates of diplomacy and justice, a Libran and Virgoan's love should be fair and true. If these two make any vows together, they will take them very seriously. However, it is not all contracts and scales in this relationship, as the Mercury-inspired Virgoan and Venus-ruled Libran could both have a shared love of beauty and crafts. A date night at a gallery or the theatre could be perfect for the art-loving couple. The Libran will have plenty of ideas, and the practical Virgoan could be the one that helps make those fancies a reality.

SCORPIO: COMPATIBILITY 5/5

Positioned two places apart on the zodiac calendar, the passionate and loyal bond between a Virgoan and Scorpian is a special one. The orderly Virgoan will value the steadiness of the fixed Scorpian, and similarly the loyal Scorpian will appreciate the faithfulness that the Virgoan is known for. With their complementary elements of water and earth and their matching negative energies, this typically introverted couple will enjoy the nourishing effects of spending quality time together. Theirs is an intimate relationship but not without some passionate arguments, thanks to the Scorpian's power-ruled influence of Pluto and the Virgoan's sharp tongue.

SAGITTARIUS: COMPATIBILITY 2/5

These two lovers may really have their work cut out for them. Whilst the outdoorsy Sagittarian and earthy Virgoan both have a strong love for being outside in nature, they have some serious core differences. The Virgoan, for example, loves routine, which the Sagittarian can't abide. Elsewhere, the wild Sagittarian, who gallops heart first towards goals, can sometimes feel too reckless for the overthinking Virgoan, whilst the Sagittarian might find the Virgoan's overactive mind to be a hindrance. If they can find some common ground, this mutable pair could experience an honest and thought-provoking relationship.

CAPRICORN: COMPATIBILITY 4/5

When a hard-working Capricornian and meticulous Virgoan fall in love, there won't be many cracks in their relationship. With the Virgoan's tool kit of practical skills and the Capricornian's portfolio of material achievements, this hard-working couple may well be best at taking on grand projects. Perhaps building their own home somewhere in the countryside would suit this couple, where their shared earth element can be appreciated at its best, and their quieter negative energies embraced. This firm relationship may lack some spontaneity, so thoughtful surprises now and again could help keep the excitement alive.

AQUARIUS: COMPATIBILITY 2/5

An idealist Aquarian and realist Virgoan may not be an obvious match, but this couple can be very happy if they find key ideas and goals to share. The organised Virgoan will appreciate the Saturn-ruled part of the Aquarian that represents structure and order, but less so the rebellious Uranus side that enjoys throwing out the rulebook. The airy Aquarian and Mercury-ruled Virgoan are both freethinkers and should be good at allowing one another room to breathe in the relationship, which both will value. Ultimately, the optimistic Aquarian and the pragmatic Virgoan will need to find a shared ambition to balance out their stark differences.

PISCES: COMPATIBILITY 5/5

Opposites on the zodiac calendar, a hands-on Virgoan and mystical Piscean make a loving match, yet life will not be without the occasional struggle. Water and earth are elements that can create beautiful things together, but in this couple the emotional Piscean and rational Virgoan could be a tricky balancing act. For example, the Piscean sometimes exhibits an elusiveness that can be attractive or frustrating to the steady Virgoan. Overall, however, these two are deep souls that can empathise and support one another probably better than any other match, and can happily and devotedly serve one another for endless days if flexibility and patience is practised by the pair. A fixed and mutable mode can be a complimentary match, so long as Virgoans don't try to bend the will of their accommodating Piscean partner. The bond that these two can share when at its best can be sincere and spiritually liberating.

FAMILY AND FRIENDS

It's hard to ruffle unflappable Virgoans, which makes them go-to confidants in times of crisis. Their wise words can be second to none thanks to their honesty and practicality, so offering advice to friends and family is a common practice. Whilst the advice of Virgoans will usually be actively sought, their candid tones can sound callous at times. Even if their intentions are pure, their sharp words can penetrate even the thickest of skins. Virgoans might think that their Cancerian and Scorpian friends have hard shells that can withstand straight talking, for example, but they will actually need to tread lightly because both can be extremely sensitive. After a time, even the most patient of people, such as Taureans, might tire of the Virgoan disapproving tone. To avoid alienating their loved ones, particularly their own children, Virgoans should try to always be constructive rather than overly critical, and give any words of advice without condemnation.

Virgoans' homes most likely reflect their impeccable taste. Their style may be minimal, but it will always be warm. They usually function best if their homes are uncluttered, so if their bedroom is looking disorderly it might be an indication that their thoughts are too. Virgoans can often have a gift for cultivating their earth element, so a house with a garden could be an important feature, whether it's to grow their own organic vegetables or prize-winning roses. Outdoor space or not, Virgoans might decide to bring the outdoors in and decorate every room with plants that will all have been carefully selected to clean polluted air or thrive on sunny windowsills.

Not ones for openly displaying their emotions, Virgoans are more likely to silently sulk until their mood passes. Despite holding stubborn grudges that sometimes feel like a life sentence, Virgoans do forgive and forget with time – as their patient and understanding family and friends will know. Learning to move past bad feeling is essential for Virgoans, as the weight of grievances can start to feel heavy after a while. Opening up to loved ones about how they feel, and letting go of any concerns about vulnerability can be an important first step towards mending any broken bonds and forging stronger friendships. Opposites on the zodiac calendar, Pisceans may well be the emotional key to unlocking the deeper feelings lingering inside of Virgoans.

The social circle of selective Virgoans may be small but strong with lifelong friendships. Whilst they love structure, they suit easy-going and energetic signs that challenge and inspire them. Creative Arians can be the best of friends to crafty Virgoans, and their balance of negative and positive energies are a complementary force that makes for a pioneering and practical alliance.

MONEY AND CAREERS

....

Being a particular star sign will not dictate certain types of career, but it can help identify potential areas for thriving in. Conversely, to succeed in the workplace, it is just as important to understand strengths and weaknesses to achieve career and financial goals.

Thanks to their earth element, some Virgoans may be attached to material objects, but these hard-working types are usually more driven by goals than they are by money. Whilst these overachievers could be destined to make fortunes by reaching the top of their professions, many are known for their thrifty spending habits. Finding sample sales and scouring the Internet for the best insurance deals, frugal Virgoans will only part with their hard-earned money wisely and are unlikely to go on a shopping splurge. Their tendency to over-analyse could leave them struggling with indecisiveness and considering the pros and cons on almost every purchase. This means plenty of time should be allowed when accompanying them on shopping trips.

Wellbeing is of utmost important to Virgoans, so careers based around healthy living could be worthwhile. One profession that they may thrive in could be as nutritionists or cooks like fellow Virgoan chef, Melissa Hemsley. However, if chopping vegetables doesn't appeal, perhaps the health calling that speaks loudest to analytical and cool-headed Virgoans is within medicine, such as becoming doctors or surgeons. Most Virgoans love to work in a neat and pristine environment, so the clinical order of a hospital could be exactly what the career doctor ordered. Whether it's for the operating table or the dinner table, Virgoans will need a clean and chaos-free workstation if they are to function at their very best.

Virgoans can be meticulous and they often excel at finding fault, so any occupation that involves careful checking and solving problems will be a good fit. Working as consultants may well be something that Virgoans come to later in life, once word of their shrewd observation and effective counsel begins to precede them. Virgoans should be wary of their perfectionist ways when striving for improvement, however, as wanting to check and double-check everything can lead to some projects never being completed. Practical-minded Virgoans could benefit from practising a more relaxed viewpoint that finished is sometimes better than perfect.

As with family, colleagues cannot be chosen. Therefore, it can be advantageous to use star signs to learn about their key characteristics and discover the best ways of working together. Born in the sixth house where service can be second nature, Virgoans often excel at both working for, as well as with, other people. Taureans and Capricornians can work doggedly with hard-working Virgoans through the most difficult of tasks, and will bond over their shared grit and determination. Arians, Leonians and Sagittarians are also potentially good workmates, and could help lighten the load with their positive flames by always encouraging their Virgoan colleagues to down tools and take a break.

HEALTH AND WELLBEING

· · · · · · · · · · · · · · · · ·

A lack of control can make Virgoans feel anxious, but it is essential that they learn to let go periodically so that they don't make life impossible for themselves and everyone around them. Always ready to give others the best of advice, Virgoans should try to listen to their own wise words. However, seeking external professional advice may also be necessary if their need for control is verging on obsessive. Virgoans notoriously love shopping lists, pros and cons lists and to-do-lists, which can quite literally be endless. Writing down worries might free up some mental space for any overactive minds. Learning to take a break may leave Virgoans pleasantly surprised that the world does not collapse when they enjoy a well-deserved day off.

Virgoans can have a reputation for being negative. In some cases this is just them being practical in their unfiltered candid way, however, sometimes it is a fair assessment and should be mended if it is affecting their happiness. An obvious solution to balance out any negative vibe is to counteract it with some feel-good positivity. Virgoans can become stuck on focusing on the negative and lose sight of the positives surrounding them, but if they take the effort to look around they are likely to be able to find something to be grateful for. It could be family or friends, a good hair day, the sun shining outside, the rain watering the garden, and so on. Spending time with optimistic Sagittarian friends or family members could also be the positive injection that Virgoans need to boost them on a down day.

Virgoans can be incredibly health conscious, and often take extra care of their mental, physical and spiritual health.

However, sometimes this can verge on hypochondria. Maybe it's because Virgoans are good at noticing the little things that makes them so alert to their bodily health, but their Internet history is probably littered with online searches desperately trying to self-diagnose the latest potential rash. Scaring themselves with Internet diagnoses is probably a common occurrence, so registering with a local doctor should be the number one priority whenever Virgoans move home. They may well be on a first-name basis before long, but they are always happy to add another name to their Christmas card list. Virgoans generally take such good care of themselves that they should hopefully not have too many reasons to visit the doctor's. Associated with the stomach, Virgoans may wish to take extra care of this area by eating a gut-friendly diet, and easing any anxieties that might be tying their insides into knots.

Virgo

....

DAILY FORECASTS
for 2021

OCTOBER

. . . .

Friday 1st

The Moon drops into your hidden sector. You may feel
emotionally drained as it opposes Saturn which can feel like a
lead weight. However, nice connections to Mars and the Sun
both in your money and values sector means that you can have
a cheery night alone if needed.

Saturday 2nd

It's possible that you feel a little tearful today. Uranus is
making you unstable as he dredges up more stuff from your
psyche. A connection to your ruler, Mercury, helps you to
process your private thoughts. Venus and Pluto help you
transform outdated ways of thinking and feeling.

Sunday 3rd

This morning the Moon enters your own sign and gives you
back personal strength. You can be methodical and rational
about deep feelings. Assessing past and future karma will keep
your mind occupied. Keep your notebook and checklists handy
as you'll need them when your mind goes into overdrive.

Monday 4th

Neptune attempts to draw you back into fantasy thinking. You
may see yourself through the eyes of another, possibly a lover
as Neptune is in your relationship sector. There may even be
a pleasant surprise there when you realise just how much you
are admired for your natural qualities.

Tuesday 5th

Transformations come easily today. The lord of change, Pluto, lets you see how a few tweaks to your current ways of thinking makes things better. This may solve a problem you've been struggling with. Venus communicates deep and intense knowledge of self-love to you. Secret yearnings rise up and are spoken aloud.

Wednesday 6th

A new moon meets Mars. This is a time to make goals about finances and values as they will surely stick. Pluto turns direct today, adding conviction to these intentions. Out with the old and in with the new. The Moon then meets Mercury retrograde who files these intentions away.

Thursday 7th

Venus glides into your family sector. Watch how she brings harmony to this area now. The Moon enters the sign she has just left and your conversations will be strange. You're emotionally drawn to talking about life's mysteries and the taboo. Secrets may be shared between siblings.

Friday 8th

The Sun and Mars meet up today making a powerhouse of energy in your finance and values sector. You cannot miss the chance to use this energy and attract cash. You may have a great new money-making scheme ready to implement. This influence can also make you show off.

Saturday 9th

Tread carefully today, as the planetary energy is wild. You may have a ghost from the past come to visit you. Arguments are likely as Mercury bumps backwards into Mars. The Moon and Venus meet to smooth this over but instead, this connection makes you vulnerable to attack.

Sunday 10th

Saturn turns direct today and this will feel like a weight off your shoulders. Someone may have been relying too heavily on you over this period. If you have been overloaded with extra obligations you will see some fall away now. Perhaps a period of struggle has come to a natural end.

Monday 11th

A happy, outgoing Moon in your family sector brings you some joy today. You may be making plans for travel or a family adventure. Keep this idea burning as it may be a future activity which will open up the world to you and your kin.

Tuesday 12th

The Moon is now in your creative sector. Step by step you're achieving a milestone. Perhaps you haven't noticed this. Art, poetry, and love affairs all take time to perfect. Is this happening now? Genius thinking gives you a heads up in the right direction. How are you different from your peers?

Wednesday 13th

Patience must be exercised today as the Moon connects to Neptune. You may be in a rush to climb a mountain but you must remember to enjoy the view. Pluto shows you what you need to strip away and lighten your load. Make each step count.

Thursday 14th

The Moon meets newly direct Saturn today. This may feel like you're stepping into the headmaster's office with anticipation. Fear not, you're going to get some praise. Venus sends you optimism and courage. Uranus' rumblings are the butterflies you feel in your stomach. Fear is an illusion today.

Friday 15th

Sun and Moon both connect to Jupiter today. Ego and emotions can be larger than life. Try to remain calm and kind as others may push your buttons and try getting you to react. Rebelliousness doesn't suit you, it will make you look like a sulky child.

Saturday 16th

Have a quiet day with a lover or an important person. The Moon is free of connections to planets but does connect to the karmic points. You may be dreamy and idealistic today and this is harmless. Reminiscing about the past fills your Saturday nicely. You can be whimsical, too.

Sunday 17th

Jupiter turns direct today. This also comes as a relief. Your health and duties sector has taken a bashing this year. Your inner voice has something to say to you today so make sure that you listen. Merging and connecting to a lover is getting easier now. Enjoy this time.

Monday 18th

Now Mercury turns direct. Your tricky ruler will retrace his steps in your finance and values sector once more. You should know by now which area you need to deal with differently. Perhaps a home makeover didn't work out quite as well as planned and needs to be redone.

Tuesday 19th

The Moon in your intimacy sector is the first to contact Mercury today. They face off and you must try to sift through emotional and logical processes. Feeling and thinking are difficult to reconcile. Mars and Jupiter both want you to err on the side of reason.

Wednesday 20th

You may be unsure how to proceed with any plans you've been harbouring for a while now. Forget those and look at what you have achieved this year. A full moon in your intimacy sector shows you if shared finances or deep relating has come to anything. Celebrate your gains.

Thursday 21st

In your travel sector, the Moon meets Uranus. It's very likely that you make an impulse purchase which is expensive or luxurious. This can include suddenly taking off for an adventure. Saturn is watching with a stern brow. You might regret this at a later date.

Friday 22nd

You are very tempted to follow an impossible dream today. Be sensible, this could be disastrous. Mars and Pluto are at odds and you don't want the planets of war and permanent endings to influence any rash decision you make now. Wait until the energy gives you a green light.

Saturday 23rd

The Sun enters your communications sector now. You will find that your everyday conversations become more interesting and light up your brain cells with many ideas. There is potential to explore the darker side of life now that the light shines on it, which could make you feel safer as you enter unknown waters.

Sunday 24th

The Moon in your career sector opposes Venus today. You may see a conflict between men and women, fathers and mothers, or workers and homemakers. When the two feminine planets face off, there's a chance that gossip and jealousy are afoot. Be mindful that this doesn't involve you.

Monday 25th

Your mind will be so busy today that you welcome a quiet retreat by evening. A late-night conversation with a close friend or a chat on social media helps you to wind down. Before you sleep you'll feel more positive but still mentally active.

Tuesday 26th

Venus and Neptune are at odds today. Families and lovers both demand your time. The best thing you can do is avoid both and enjoy time to yourself or with your online friends. You must protect your energy and stay in your comfort zone or risk being angered and defensive.

Wednesday 27th

Another difficult day. You may see control issues or power struggles coming from your love affairs. Speak up clearly and show them the boundaries. Your heart needs you to lie low with familiar things around you whilst your head is busy trying to keep the peace with people close to you.

Thursday 28th

The energy picks up and you are allowed some peace. The Moon enters your private sector where for once you enjoy the silence. You have no need to roar and be heard. Venus and Jupiter combine to quieten your family and other obligations or at least make them joyful.

Friday 29th

Whilst in your private sector, the Moon reflects light on your dark areas. You aren't too happy about dealing with this today. Gentle whisperings from your ruler Mercury enable you to sift through them and decide which are necessary and which to deal with at another time.

Saturday 30th

Mars enters your communications sector. You will be driven and forceful with him here. There will be no stone unturned and no secret left preserved. In his own sign, he is ruthless. You can do all your detective work now and get to the bottom of the deepest mystery.

Sunday 31st

The Moon is in your sign and you're a force to be reckoned with today. The selfless servant of everyone is taking a stand. Watch whose noses you put out of joint now as this will tell you a lot about who takes you for granted. Say what you mean now.

NOVEMBER

. . . .

Monday 1st

Your mind is on fire today. Mercury and Jupiter connect to help you get things in order on a grand scale. Neptune beckons you to switch off but you ignore the call and multi-task like a professional. Changes or endings can be made now with very little regret.

Tuesday 2nd

Forward motion might be hindered by something unforeseen today. You may have to rethink a strategy or find balance in another way. Saturn watches how you handle this and gives you the benefit of wisdom to deal with this in a responsible, adult way. It will all turn out well.

Wednesday 3rd

Pluto is still influencing your mood and productivity today. You may feel emotionally attached to something you need to let go. This could be money, investments or property. The Moon and Mercury have a chat and you'll need to dissociate feelings from logic and reason. Jupiter makes your emotions larger.

Thursday 4th

A new moon in your communications sector asks you to do the detective work necessary. This is a tricky day with a lot of planetary energies which can make you unstable. Venus is about to leave your family sector. You must get to the root of any problems now.

Friday 5th

The Sun sits opposite Uranus today. This acts like a light bulb moment where you get clarity and maybe a genius solution to a difficult situation. Mercury flies into your communications sector where he will be your best ally. Expect a lot of deep conversations and short trips now.

Saturday 6th

Enjoy this weekend with family. Elders need your love and attention and you will be happy to give it. A love affair may be starting for you. Mercury talks to Venus the planet of love who is in your creative sector now. Expressions of love come easily.

Sunday 7th

You may feel that you have a lot of duties now but remember that you have also shed some. Family comes first today, and you approach all that you need to do with optimism and joy. Your altruistic nature comes out, making you happy to serve those who need you.

Monday 8th

The Moon is making amazing connections today. She sits in your creative sector generating energy, conversations, love and surprise moments. This is a lucky day for you. Your divine essence shines through and you attract all the right people. Fill your heart and let it overflow to others.

Tuesday 9th

You may struggle with issues of control as the Moon meets Pluto. However, this could highlight a need to check in with your emotions. You have let a lot go recently, perhaps you are just pausing to think about how that makes you feel. Neptune lets you listen to your inner voice.

Wednesday 10th

Mercury and Mars meet up and their effect has you running around at full speed. Chores, messages and visits are all achieved easily with these two behind you. You may not like it very much and will vocalise this to whoever listens. Be productive and don't sulk.

Thursday 11th

The Moon meets Jupiter today. You could be blowing your own trumpet and inflating yourself with pride. Showing off about how much you can do with efficiency isn't a good idea. You are noticed and appreciated for what you do, there's no need to point it out.

Friday 12th

Your lover or special person will need your attention over the weekend. This is an excellent time to switch off and enjoy some downtime. You may feel at a crossroads, but this is a passing phase and will be over soon. Venus wants you to merge with your lover or spirit.

Saturday 13th

You may contemplate the acts of surrender and sacrifice and what they mean to you in a partnership. Your sexual energy and art of conversation are both on a roll. You can win someone over now. Be careful not to talk about risky subjects too soon.

Sunday 14th

After a time of connection, you desire to make plans and strategies to merge deeper. You may need to slow down. Be mindful of personal boundaries and don't push another person out of their comfort zone. Tread carefully and keep your plans on the back-burner for a later date.

Monday 15th

It's likely that you see conflict arise between men and women today. Egos and emotions are not in sync with traditional gender roles, causing disturbances or bullying between the sexes. This is in your more personal areas of life and not your wider world. Remember to be responsible and respectful.

Tuesday 16th

The battles continue to occur in your intimate and love sectors. Jupiter tries to help by connecting to the Moon and asking you to see out the truth of a matter. Jupiter loves justice and sits in your health and duties sector. A wise elder may give impartial advice today.

Wednesday 17th

With Mars and Uranus in opposition, anything could happen.
Your sectors of communication and travel will be explosive
today as these two volatile planets face off. This could be an all-
out war or highly productive time. Either way, protect yourself
from the fall-out and try not to get exhausted.

Thursday 18th

The Moon is now involved in this war. You will be emotionally
charged and may need to reluctantly take a side. You ask for
help from Neptune, beg him to take you away from it all. You
may wish to shut the door and wrap yourself up in a blanket.

Friday 19th

A full moon in your travel sector appears to be the culmination
of the recent difficult energy. You can make a last-ditch
attempt to detach yourself from other people's dramas. Treat
yourself with tasty exotic food and remind yourself of your
desire to travel. Set your mind onto a different path.

Saturday 20th

Have a day with your thoughts. The Moon in your career
sector gives you space and time to process a lot of information
today. You may be researching for work or pleasure. Mercury
whispers something to Jupiter in your duties sector, he says
he's not available to others today.

Sunday 21st

Your mind is still busy. You may be following many different threads of enquiry. Don't take on too many as you will become overloaded and ultimately indecisive. You attend only to the most important of duties today. Let them be the ones that make you smile.

Monday 22nd

The Sun moves into your vibrant family sector today. Expect the seasonal festivities to begin now. You're protective of your energy and only allow those who you are very close to break down your barriers. Social activities may drain you as you are somewhat vulnerable to attack.

Tuesday 23rd

You're being called out of hiding by a potential lover. You desire to respond but need to hide out a little longer. This stirs your sexual energy and will keep you at just the right temperature until the time is right. Make do with fantasies and dreams for now.

Wednesday 24th

Mercury is at the final degree of your communications sector. If you need to make contact, then it's crucial that you do so now. You must step out of your cave and be bold. This evening the Moon shifts into your private sector which is ruled by courageous Leo.

Thursday 25th

Don't back out of any plans which take you beyond your comfort zone, they will do you good. Venus and Mars are close to making a great connection between your communications and creative sector. This energy is too good to miss. Find your best clothes and get ready.

Friday 26th

The Moon opposes Jupiter while in your hidden sector. You may have a moment of crisis and believe that you're not worthy or not good enough. This is fear talking, don't listen. You're being given the opportunity to shine in all your glory, take it.

Saturday 27th

The Moon dips into your sign and your confidence rises. However, your communications are lacking the fire to back this up. Use your Virgo powers and make a checklist. Prepare a speech with crib notes if necessary. Check every detail of any plan put forward to you now.

Sunday 28th

The butterflies in your stomach are making you twitchy. Fantasy driven Neptune calls you from your relationship sector, but you're refusing to go there. You feel much safer in your own territory. Stick with it, this nervous energy will dissipate soon and you will be grounded once more.

Monday 29th

You feel much more balanced today and the voices in your
head are calmed. This is due to Mercury, your chatty ruler,
being in the heat of the Sun. This is a good time to listen
to the one, true, guiding voice and ignore your inner critic.
Amorous Mars is ready for love.

Tuesday 30th

Today you may be more moody than usual. The Moon
makes an unhelpful connection to Venus and you may be
overemotional. This will pass quickly. Many other planetary
connections suggest that the energy is right for you to enjoy
some fun, laughter and love. You deserve this.

DECEMBER
· · · · · · · · · · · · · · · · · ·

Wednesday 1st

Neptune turns direct today. This is great news if you've been too idealistic and unrealistic in your partnerships. You will now have clarity and see falsity dissolve before your eyes. You may have been wearing rose-tinted glasses or projecting your own issues onto another. This will be exposed.

Thursday 2nd

A deeply communicative Moon makes you do all the right research and investigations about highly sensitive subjects. There is much you want to know and learn. Be careful that you don't probe too deeply as you wander into sensitive areas you're not ready for.

Friday 3rd

Mars and the Moon meet up today. Sex drive is high and a romantic evening is likely. However, this can also lead to passive-aggression. The Moon squares off with Jupiter so be mindful that you don't push boundaries too far. By evening you are more family orientated but still outgoing and cheerful.

Saturday 4th

A new moon in your family sector is a great chance to check in with your loved ones and make sure everyone is OK. There may be members who need their spirits lifted. You wear your heart on your sleeve today and whatever comes out of your mouth is truly heartfelt.

Sunday 5th

Your mood is buoyant, and you're ready for anything that is thrown at you. This afternoon, you slow down and decide that any progression in your creative sector, including love affairs, needs to be taken one step at a time. This is not a bad thing.

Monday 6th

You're determined and steadfast today. Taking a good look at all your responsibilities is time well spent. You can be highly organised as the Moon makes helpful connections to planets which are usually distracting or volatile. Mars and Pluto connect to help you tear down old values.

Tuesday 7th

The Moon now connects to both Pluto and Mars. They are clearing the way for new ways of thinking, creating and relating to come in. The Moon shifts into your health and duties sector. Check in with your body now and do something for yourself. Assess your diet and exercise regimes.

Wednesday 8th

Today may be tricky as you come up against conflict from an elder or boss. This energy could also mean that you're being too hard on yourself, you are your own boss after all. You may not feel so good. Tears and tantrums may not be far away.

Thursday 9th

Have you possibly burnt out? The Moon meets Jupiter but also squares off with Mars. Your energy may be depleted. Take some time to pause and be good to yourself. A family member may offer advice. Listen to what they have to say, it will be valuable.

. . . .

Friday 10th

The Moon floats into your relationship sector giving you a chance to switch off and relax with a loved one. Simple energy allows you to treat both of you to a tasty dinner or a great film. You're restless but in a nice way. This means that something has touched you.

Saturday 11th

Venus and Pluto meet in your creative sector. You will likely see control issues and power struggles today. Other Moon connections suggest that you take an objective view and do nothing. Detach yourself from the drama and let others deal with it. Don't speak your mind today.

Sunday 12th

Venus and Pluto are still having trouble agreeing today. Are you too attached to something which needs to change or be ended? What is it you're trying to hang on to? Take a peek into your relationship sector as the Sun is making a tough connection to Neptune's illusions.

Monday 13th

Mercury enters your creative sector with many ideas and words of love. Mars also changes signs. He marches into your family sector. He will pull up the stragglers and get everyone ready for an adventure. The Moon makes you emotionally deep and intense but with lots of ideas for intimate evenings.

Tuesday 14th

Your travel sector is highlighted and you feel that familiar pull towards unknown territory. Have you had a holiday this year? Perhaps you're regretting not getting away often enough. You fill your mind with far-reaching plans to visit lands that can tantalise your senses.

Wednesday 15th

You're restless today. Elders or people in authority may be giving you some pressure. When the Moon meets Uranus that pressure is likely to blow up in your face. Toe the line and concentrate on your work. Do what it takes to get through the day without conflict.

Thursday 16th

Today you find a way to make those difficult changes or let attachments go. Neptune helps you to dissolve any illusions you've been harbouring whilst Venus sends you love and peace to do so. Take it slowly and process your feelings. You will soon see the benefits of this.

Friday 17th

Your mind is extra busy. Maybe you're bringing work home with you for the weekend. This will cause friction with your family time and you will need to find a happy balance. Stay disciplined and alert today and over the weekend. Keep emotions away from rational decisions now.

Saturday 18th

Neptune is asking you to switch off, but you cannot spare the time. If you're to enjoy the festivities then you must do the extra work now. This isn't easy at this time of year. You may have to decline a party invitation and keep your mind on your tasks.

Sunday 19th

Venus turns retrograde today. This will be a period where love affairs are disrupted, and you may see a face from the past return. A full moon in your career sector highlights all that you have been working towards this year. The extra work has paid off.

Monday 20th

The Moon in your social sector brings some light relief. It opposes Mercury who asks you to mind your words and not risk upsetting friends. Alcohol can loosen tongues and cause problems. As Uranus is involved here too, let his restlessness bring a good time and not conflict.

Tuesday 21st

The winter solstice occurs today. This is a time to pause and reflect on the year gone by. Try to find a pivot and maintain balance if just for now. The days will shorten and the darker months are upon you. How will you fill up the long, dark nights?

Wednesday 22nd

The Moon is in your hidden sector. You may need to have some time alone and recharge ready for the upcoming celebrations. Family members may try to call you out of hiding but you must decline. Do only what is necessary and keep your energy for the next few days.

Thursday 23rd

Jupiter has come back to the final degree of your health and duties sector. This planet of joy and expansion asks that you have gone as far as you can go in this area. How is your health? Are you mentally well or exhausted? Make a note to review this.

Friday 24th

The Moon drops into your sign this morning. You will find that you're required for your organising skills. This may cause you some grief as you feel you're being taken for granted. Make sure that you have the energy to comply or you will not enjoy the celebrations.

Saturday 25th

Control issues and power struggles are most evident today. Venus has met Pluto again in your creative sector. You may have to surrender the control to someone just to keep the peace. Don't sacrifice yourself, just go with the flow and do what is asked of you.

Sunday 26th

You're emotionally involved with the power struggles in your creative sector but you're handling them well. The Moon in your sign makes good connections. It's possible that you're taking charge and being as objective. Your keen eye for detail may save the day.

Monday 27th

The Moon is in your finances and value sector. You know your worth and are able to get this across to others today. You can be strict and assertive without upsetting anyone. You may be called on for your wisdom in making balanced decisions about money. Be responsible and don't overspend.

Tuesday 28th

You will need to be firm but fair with someone today. The Moon makes hard connections to the planets in your creative sector. This is another day where you must stand up for your right to be who you are without filters. Venus and Pluto make it challenging.

Wednesday 29th

The Moon in your communications sector gives you trouble speaking to authority figures today. There is a possibility of a tantrum or an upsetting episode where you don't get your own way. Look to your own behaviour and own it. Lucky Jupiter enters your relationship sector for the next year.

Thursday 30th

You have the gift of the gab and can talk anyone around to your way of thinking today. Mercury meets Pluto and as your ruler, he assists you in being persuasive. You can do this with love and compassion and avoid unnecessary conflict. Well done.

Friday 31st

The end of the year is here. The Moon sits with the point of past karma and you look back at how much you've lost and achieved this year. The Moon also meets Mars and gives you the emotional energy to party all night and see the new year in.

Virgo

. . . .

DAILY FORECASTS
for 2022

JANUARY

. . . .

Saturday 1st

Happy New Year and welcome to 2022. Your year begins on a quiet note. You may be winding down with close family and planning adventures for the year. Love relationships may be exciting and filled with anticipation. Take things slowly and simply enjoy their company. Find pleasure in being open and honest with each other.

Sunday 2nd

A new moon is a great chance to set goals and intentions around creative and romantic pursuits. A long-term project or joint venture may appeal. This could be the year that you scale new heights if you stay dedicated and work hard. Discover what mutual visions you share. What would you like to learn?

Monday 3rd

A ghost from the past may tug on your heartstrings. This is a cue to release a connection which no longer serves you. You have much to look forward to and old cords need to be cut. Life is shifting and you don't need to take excess baggage on your journey.

Tuesday 4th

Your head and heart are in talks today. You may hear your inner critic, but listen carefully as you may also hear words of encouragement and inspiration. Duty and responsibility to others pull you back to your centre. Do what needs to be done with a clear conscience.

Wednesday 5th

An open heart and sense of adventure get you through the day. Family issues may need your drive and energy to get things done. It could be that you're leading the way or promoting values that you're passionate about. Your optimistic outlook attracts others to your cause.

Thursday 6th

Partner time can be dreamy and floaty, and you may do something which fills both your hearts. Jupiter is in your relationship area bringing many blessings. You may be truth-seeking and expanding the world you share together. Food, pleasure, philosophies and culture can make your partnership rich and meaningful now.

Friday 7th

If coming down to earth is difficult, hold on to your inner compass. You have a great sense of where your life is heading and can be guided by checking in frequently. There may be outside conflict to deal with, but stay true to your personal path without self-sacrificing or submitting.

Saturday 8th

If you have itchy feel today, try to get out and about. Unusual activities can freshen up a dull routine. Maybe you can plan to tick something off your bucket list. You may be in the right mood to make enquiries. This is a good time to start an exercise regime.

Sunday 9th

You may hit a stumbling block which puts your plans on hold. An old love or attachment may be barring your progress. Perhaps you haven't let go completely. You may be side-tracked this evening as family or home need your energy and commitment to make something happen.

Monday 10th

Today you must aim to focus on one thing that can be achieved over time. Put down roots and stop hesitating. You have the necessary conviction to make a dream come true. This is a new journey and you will need to take a leap of faith. Trust that all will be well.

Tuesday 11th

Inspiration flows and you may have emotional reactions to bright ideas. Be mindful that you don't get distracted from your daily mundane chores. Focus on what needs to be done or you may be playing catch up this evening. You may resent not having time to dream today.

Wednesday 12th

A compassionate heart opens you to receive divine messages and keep you on course. You may be more romantic today and you fully understand that remaining rooted and laying solid foundations can make your love and creative endeavours prosper. Endings, beginnings and permanent changes are easier now as you are more accepting.

Thursday 13th

Use your mental faculties today. You may have a busy mind and could be attempting to solve a problem regarding your place in the wider world. This may take some time as your ruler, Mercury, is due to retrograde. Do your research and back up all your devices. Make sure that communications at work are clear.

Friday 14th

Mercury turns retrograde in your health and duties zone. You may wish to ensure that your diet is good and health appointments are all up to date. You may find time for introspection now and could be reviewing issues of duty and service to your community.

Saturday 15th

It's possible that you feel tired today and wish to keep a low profile. A few close friends or family can provide a comfort zone. Keep your bubble small and make sure that you are nurtured and nourished with good company. Intuition may be high, so listen to what it says.

Sunday 16th

You may get a moment of revelation today. This could be a light bulb switching on which can transform old issues into something of greater value. You may also experience passive aggression or a pull to a past love which unsettles you. Watch your words and actions. You are more sensitive now.

Monday 17th

A full moon highlights issues of control and manipulation. You might deal with this by getting defensive or crumbling under pressure. However, if you can be strong and protect your values, you may notice that your challenger loses interest. Don't be coerced into conflict or power struggles.

Tuesday 18th

Uranus turns direct today. You may have an urge to break free and travel the world in the next few months. Radical or unconventional cultures may interest you more. Take time this evening to process your own thoughts and avoid getting into petty squabbles. Put any thoughts on paper and scrutinise them.

Wednesday 19th

You could be super stubborn now and insist on your privacy or your own way. Keep your personal boundaries strong and respect those of other people too. If you're being asked to step up and contribute to a group cause, consider whether it is in alignment with your core values.

Thursday 20th

This is a good time to look at any health issues you may have neglected recently. The Moon drops into your sign and you may be more inclined to declutter your life. You could start a job which becomes too big by evening and wish you hadn't bothered.

Friday 21st

Grounded practical energy may help you deal with tricky issues today. Use a methodical approach and be analytical. As a Virgo, you leave no stone unturned and this is a skill which can steer you away from trouble. Stick to this way of dealing with unwanted intrusions which refuse to go away.

Saturday 22nd

You may wake up with a fuzzy head today, but once this is cleared, you may have a productive day. You could be de-cluttering or transforming a workspace. You may also be putting down ground rules or first steps in relationships. Express yourself well and set reasonable standards.

Sunday 23rd

Your ruler Mercury is in the heart of the Sun today. You must listen carefully as you may receive important guidance or a new mission. Your mind may be doing overtime balancing expectations or getting a reality check. A last minute effort or urgent action may be required within your family life.

Monday 24th

Your energy for romance and creativity picks up and will remain so for some weeks. Now is the time to initiate a long-term project which can be successful. You could be mourning a loss this evening, but this may simply be a small regret that you didn't implement it sooner.

Tuesday 25th

Take it easy today. The planetary energy may trigger many emotions, and this may be intense. Feelings and conversations are affected by Mercury and as your ruler, you may need to listen out for the lesson here. Conversations can be tricky; clarity evades you and you feel all of this deeply.

Wednesday 26th

Tensions may be high now and you could be struggling a little with romance or artistic projects. Know that this won't last long, and you just have to ride it. Something is brewing under the surface and making you uneasy. Don't attempt to investigate areas not meant for you.

Thursday 27th

A karmic tie to the past may throw you off course now. Let it go, release it and move on. Family bonds can be supportive now and keep you on a straight path. Fluctuating emotions may be unsettling this evening, so find a way of grounding yourself or keeping busy.

Friday 28th

You may have a keen sense of your personal boundaries and limits today. If you're asked to take on something new, consider it carefully. Although it may seem like a worthy, respectful choice, it may also be a cause for extra stress and declining health. Don't commit to anything just yet.

Saturday 29th

Stay alert today. You may experience something unexpected which can shock you to your core. Venus turns direct and this may release some pressure you've been feeling regarding old loves and projects. This afternoon your energy picks up and you may get sexy or emotionally attached to a love interest.

Sunday 30th

Be with the one you love today. Your heart is feeling lighter and more harmonised. You may have freed space within to truly be present with a partner. Little shocks to your body and system may be exciting and you may feel in tune with your inner compass.

Monday 31st

You may not be out of the woods just yet. If you can't walk your talk, stay still. There may be some retrograde mishaps if you have misunderstood someone's intentions. Be respectful and don't try pushing buttons. Helping others can be most rewarding today. Unconditional love can work both ways.

FEBRUARY

. . . .

Tuesday 1st

The new moon today is a great way to set intentions and lay
down boundaries. You may be thinking about doing more in
your community or helping a worthy cause. However, you
must think hard as you could be taking on more than you can
manage, and it will become a burden.

Wednesday 2nd

Love and romance are featured now. Be careful that you don't
drift off to a fantasy island with unrealistic expectations. You
could be assertive and driven enough to take a relationship
to new heights or depths. You may also project your own
fantasies and be totally misguided by them.

Thursday 3rd

However, you feel today will be highly exaggerated. This can
be in a good way but can also mean that you're being over-
imaginative and creating impossible quests for yourself. Say
grounded and take off any rose-coloured spectacles. It's unfair
to put someone on a pedestal as it is far to fall.

Friday 4th

Mercury turns direct now. You may have a better idea of what's
real and what's not. Your passions can be returned full fold if
you're open, honest and realistic. You may be willing to go
the extra mile for a partner, but you must ensure that they
want this too.

Saturday 5th

You may be tempted to force an issue today, but you must hold back. You could do more harm than good if you persist. Look at the long-term consequences and how it fits in with your daily life. One can't live on a floating island full time.

Sunday 6th

You may feel thwarted in an attempt to move things along. Use this setback as a positive thing and observe your emotional attachment to speed and urgency. It could be that you're jumping important steps, and this will only lead to disaster. Stick to the rules and move at a slower pace.

Monday 7th

Grounding energy is more helpful to you now. You may have worked out a solution or discarded an impulse to run before you can walk. Hard work and determination will be more beneficial to you. Goals will be reached in their own time and you may appreciate this more today.

Tuesday 8th

There's something you just can't get to grips with today. This may involve travel, education or other subjects about the wider world. Try not to push through this issue as your blocks are teaching you that there are steps or initiations you need to master first.

Wednesday 9th

Use your mind to do research or negotiations now. This is a great time for getting chores done in the workplace. Your mind is keen, and you can look at many angles before committing to one. Do your homework and make sure you have all the facts in front of you.

Thursday 10th

Stay away from anything which may drain your energy today and keep focusing on facts. Logic and reason are your best allies and resources at work. There may be decisions to make which require you to have a level head. People turn to you for alternative thinking. You can be most articulate today.

Friday 11th

Be practical today. You may have a swift change of mind regarding an opinion or creative project. There may be small tweaks needed to completely transform something that has been troubling you. Listen out for hints, wisdom or advice as you may receive another mission from your ruler Mercury.

Saturday 12th

You may be feeling particularly romantic and driven to connect today. The celestial lovers Mars and Venus are getting close. This means that you may have a desire to merge passion and beauty, drive and harmony, masculine and feminine to create something outstanding. Find your muse and let inspiration flow.

Sunday 13th

Moments of self-doubt could creep into your awareness now. This is a passing phase and simply indicates that you could be fearful of having something special destroyed before it has been born. You may be sensitive to criticism and prefer to retreat rather than put yourself in the firing line.

Monday 14th

As the lovers edge even closer to each other, your emotions may be off the scale. Anticipation may be unbearable. What is about to be birthed into the world is very precious to you. Stick to your guns and be patient. You can announce it very soon and be proud of yourself.

Tuesday 15th

You may have more restless energy than you know what to do with. Try doing something practical or relaxing. A walk in nature or physical exercise may suffice. You have a lot to process in your mind now and you may benefit from calming it before expressing yourself.

Wednesday 16th

Mars and Venus meet and there are fireworks. A full moon accompanies them and throws light into your darkest corners. You may notice a revelation, a sense of relief or a feeling of old wounds being healed once and for all. Make the most of this wonderful energy and create beauty.

Thursday 17th

The Moon in your sign brings you back to your sensible, introspective self. Your natural ability to analyse and look within brings you back down to earth. You may feel a change from your very roots and be eager to let the whole world know about it.

Friday 18th

The lovely energy continues to make you feel great. There is so much potential waiting for you to access and create masterpieces. Your entire demeanour may give away how you're feeling, and others may wish to get a piece of it. Concentrate on your loved one this evening.

Saturday 19th

Today, it may become clear that what you value most are equality and harmony. You may be enjoying this with a partner or taking time to freshen up and clean your home environment. Money matters could be healthy now. Make sure that your body and mind are also fit and well.

Sunday 20th

A passing Moon phase may give you some doubts this afternoon. Pay no attention, there is nothing wrong. This may be your own insecurities creeping to the surface. It's okay to feel fearful, but take a moment to stand outside yourself and look in. You will see how valued you are.

Monday 21st

Conversations may develop a probing or intense edge. There's so much emotional energy surrounding love, relationships and getting to know someone that you may feel this intensely and be swept away. This is truly a transformational time for you, so embrace it and probe as deeply as you wish.

Tuesday 22nd

This is a delicious time of connection on a grand scale. Your creative pursuits will prosper, and your romance may reach a level way beyond your understanding. This may be what your inner compass is guiding you towards. Your higher self knows what you need and is steering your course.

Wednesday 23rd

Today you have a chance to release emotional baggage or karma before spreading your wings to fly. Family and close friends may feel left behind as you soar high above them and can't be caught. They will understand in time when they see how happy your life is right now.

Thursday 24th

Go with the flow today, however difficult this is. You may wish to follow a course which is too big for you at the moment. Recognising your personal boundaries and limits will be useful and can stop you from doing anything impulsive and silly. You still have mundane duties to attend to.

Friday 25th

You may feel resentful this morning as you can't quite catch your dreams. This is frustrating but is a way to ensure that your family duties remain a priority. This afternoon you can look forward to more time and energy with your art, music or lover.

Saturday 26th

Your emotions and ego are in sync now. With Mars and Venus still together, this can mean that you feel more of a whole person than a fragmented collection of parts. Travel and higher education plans may be made and can be exciting. Perhaps you need to take a literal journey too.

Sunday 27th

There is incredibly special planetary energy for you to access today. Be with our muse, your passions and your lover. Express yourself without filters. Let others see how you may have transformed simply by flowing your dreams and visions. Be there for them and they will be there for you.

Monday 28th

This is a great day for discussing shared visions with a partner. You may discover what you want to invest in together. The pleasures of life are there for you to indulge in. Make sure that you're both in agreement and ready to travel the road together.

MARCH
· · · · · · · · · · · · · · · · ·

Tuesday 1st

Expect the unexpected today and you may be pleasantly
surprised. You may find that your outside world is getting
bigger and inviting you to explore it. The Moon enters your
partner zone and continues to fill your heart with dreamy,
floaty emotions. Have a great ride and enjoy this tide of love.

Wednesday 2nd

Things are changing rapidly. You may be swept away in a tide
of inexplicable joy. A new moon in your relationship zone gives
you a chance to set beautiful, poetic and charming goals. Make
sure that any new quest is attainable. Don't go chasing a holy
grail as you'll be disappointed.

Thursday 3rd

Whatever happens today can considerably change your life
for the better. Old and outdated habits or conditioning may
be swept away and leave you space for new growth. This is
like getting an upgrade and jumping up a level towards your
higher self and spirit. A significant change has a new meaning.

Friday 4th

You may be a little exhausted today. Your emotions have been
enjoying a roller-coaster ride. Now they need more direction.
You may think about making plans, but beware of making
them too flaky and intangible. Also, be sure not to make too
many, it's best to focus on one.

Saturday 5th

Another day of blessings rains down on you. You may wonder if your heart will truly burst. Mars and Venus are locked in an embrace which can seal a deal in romance, art or self-expression for you. Limits are what keeps you safe from drifting into fantasy land. Respect them.

Sunday 6th

The celestial lovers move into another area of life together. You may notice that you have more compassion and a warrior spirit which may benefit you in your daily duties. You may be fighting for a worthy cause or learning to say no to people who don't recognise your boundaries.

Monday 7th

You may act like a child today and may be bouncing around with excitement. Find a way to expel excess energy and keep your good spirits up. A fun physical activity with a partner may suffice. Planning a vacation together would also be good. Don't push too far if there is a disagreement.

Tuesday 8th

A small stumbling block may present itself and you need to have a tricky conversation. It could be that someone has overstepped the mark and caused upset. Use words to smooth this over and all should be well by bedtime. Listening to another point of view helps.

Wednesday 9th

Mental activity may be draining now. You may be trying to fit too much in and burning the candle at both ends. Prioritise your duties first. When all your mundane obligations are met your mind will be free to dream extensively. Use your imagination and remember how to laugh.

Thursday 10th

It's possible that your communication within important relationships can move things up another notch. Getting to know someone may mean asking a lot of probing questions. You may become more poetic and inspired by your love. Watch out that you don't breach a boundary and dig too deeply with your enquiries.

Friday 11th

You may wish to be tucked up safely with close friends and family this weekend. Prepare for this by getting in your favourite foods and contact the people who, outside of your love relationship, nurture you. Close friends would love to hear how you're doing right now.

Saturday 12th

You may be in for a surprise which adds to your feelings of home comfort today. This could be a holiday plan or a documentary which feeds your soul and longing for foreign travel. You may think about a working holiday in which you can do some good in the wider world.

Sunday 13th

Open your eyes wide and look for your inner compass. It might be blatantly obvious and right there for you. Suddenly, it may be clear what you're meant to be doing now. Your personal path is opening up and you have the guidebook. Don't worry about other's opinions.

Monday 14th

You may be feeling down now, and self-doubt could creep in.
Let this feeling through and acknowledge it, but don't react.
You may be sitting with your private thoughts and listening to
your inner critic who has the loudest voice. Ignore it and listen
to your heart which is full of love.

Tuesday 15th

Blockages appear on your path, but look closer as they may not
be as big or as permanent as you think. Take this time of pause
to reflect on things. There's no need for action now. Just sit
still and observe where you are and where you're about to go.

Wednesday 16th

Do some fact-checking today. If you're having doubts, go
through all the paperwork and do your research. Be methodical
and remove anything from your life which is messy, uncertain
or plain nonsense. Cleaning things up physically can bring you
a sense of calm and give you more clarity.

Thursday 17th

You may feel as if the odds are stacked against you now.
Watch what you say as you may be at risk of causing an upset.
Be kind, honest and respectful. There may be a problem
which can only be solved with good communication skills.
Put dreams to one side and deal with this.

Friday 18th

A full moon in your sign can be scary as it puts you in the spotlight. You may have come to a turning point and all eyes are on you. There could be some reckoning to do as a balance may have been tipped too far one way.

Saturday 19th

Using compassion and understanding, you may take a leap into the unknown. Being hesitant is understandable, but you must trust that this will be right for you. By evening you will know that you made the right choice and equilibrium has been restored. The world awaits your contribution now.

Sunday 20th

The spring equinox arrives, and you may sense this as a coiled spring waiting for release. However, you may have already sprung into action and are now heading straight towards your goals. You could be more emotionally attached to your future than you know. Intense emotions may startle you.

Monday 21st

Your mind may be doing overtime today. The trick is not to let it turn in a negative direction. Deep feelings may be unsettling and bring back memories of old wounds. You may remember times where your good nature was taken for granted. You must trust that this is not a repeat of that.

Tuesday 22nd

Karmic situations may return, but these may be only in your mind. Your inner critic is talking, and you should stop listening. Positive change is happening, so get to grips with it. Family members may be supportive this evening if you need to let off steam.

Wednesday 23rd

Turn your attention towards what is currently going right for you. Discussions with a partner may remind you of a shared vision and entice you back into that floaty, dreamy world of your inner compass and core values. Reach out and go after what you want, it's yours for the taking.

Thursday 24th

Your emotions may fluctuate today, and you may need to spend some time alone to process this. A partner may not be helping much right now. Family members may also be distracting or not understanding. Late evening may be best for writing things down and analysing how you feel.

Friday 25th

It may be difficult for you to fix on any one thing today. Keep trying as practical application such as making art, writing or returning to the manual will eventually provide you with a breakthrough moment. Remember that dedication and determination are key to realising your dreams as this is how you function best.

Saturday 26th

Your mood lifts today and you see the benefit of allowing yourself time to work constructively. Discussions with a partner may reveal the final key to making your vision a reality. First, you must look at what is holding you back and get rid of it.

Sunday 27th

Move to a more mental attitude now. Put your plans into motion with a clear mind and strategy. Sit, down write an action plan and keep your vision big, but your steps small and achievable. You don't want to overwhelm yourself and start your anxieties building out of proportion again.

Monday 28th

You have some relief today as you return to a sense of calm. Your drive, compassion and need for harmony help you to put boundaries in place. A better sense of your personal limits lets you make a plan that is tailored towards your own needs and not those of others not involved.

Tuesday 29th

Partner time is highlighted now, and you may jump on that floating island and relax. Make sure that you keep one foot on the ground now as there's a real danger of you both isolating yourselves and never rejoining the real world again.

Wednesday 30th

Your dreamworld may be off the scale today. You will need to ensure that you are being realistic about your goals. Your heart may be swelling with love and fantasy thinking and this is lovely, but sooner or later you will come back down to earth with a bump.

Thursday 31st

Today you may be fired up with inspiration. The world is wide open for you to conquer, but you may desire to seek the deeper mysteries of life first. You can be philosophical and intrigued by ancient knowledge. Are you getting ahead of yourself? Keep it simple.

APRIL
. . . .

Friday 1st

Your head and heart are in sync now. You have a passion that is spurring you on to learn all you can about a certain person or to dig deeper into life's mysteries. A new moon can help you make a plan of action which can be both thrilling and scary.

Saturday 2nd

If you're willing to go the extra mile today, you may see that your heart opens to such an extent that altruism and love flow naturally. You may need to implement a small change before rooting any ideas firmly in reality. Speak your mind respectfully if there's a chance of conflict.

Sunday 3rd

Watch carefully for dream messages, symbols or coincidences. This is your ruler Mercury's way of communicating to you. You may find a guide or teacher who can show you the door you need to go through. Trust in this and know that there's no going back. Onwards and upwards now.

Monday 4th

You may need to deal with too many mundane routines today. This may be frustrating as you're not getting any pleasure from them. Your mood wants tactile and sensual experiences with no mental effort required. See to the daily grind and leave time for play this evening.

Tuesday 5th

A sleepless night may have been the result of your needs not being met. However, as Venus enters your relationship zone you have a promise of more beauty and pleasure to come. For now, use your mental abilities at work and filter your thought processes. You are needed and valued for this skill.

Wednesday 6th

You may not mind using logic and reason today as it flows easier. Perhaps you're the best person for the job and you take pride in this. You may be negotiating like a professional or leading a team into a new phase of work. Research and fact-finding are favoured.

Thursday 7th

Success and notability are highlighted now. The trick is to keep your mind on the job and not to drift into fantasy thinking. This may take a lot of energy and by the end of the day, you would do best to nurture yourself with close friends or family around you.

Friday 8th

Remember that you have needs too and promise yourself a treat or reward to end the day. You might look forward to binge-watching a favourite TV show or some study on future travels. Good food and a pamper treatment will also feed your soul and nourish your body.

Saturday 9th

Invitations from your social groups may entice you out for
an event or get together. This can be enjoyable as it touches
on your dreams and visions which some of your friends
may share. Add in your love partner and you may be in for a
sensitive, ethereal weekend.

Sunday 10th

Today you may want your own way and that could be a day
to yourself. You may just want to dance around your kitchen
in your pyjamas, make messy art or enjoy a day where you're
the star of your own show. This may not go down too well
with a partner.

Monday 11th

Be careful today as your energy could still be on the hectic
side. You may need to let off steam somehow. Long-distance
communications may be troublesome, and you may have to
agree to disagree. On the plus side, you have many blessings
to access in your love life.

Tuesday 12th

Trouble with an authority figure is possible today. You may
have a stroppy attitude which isn't helping. Pushing your own
agenda won't work. Give up and enjoy what is good in your
life. Later in the day, you may be humbled as you feel more
like yourself and need practical application to calm you.

Wednesday 13th

Your dreams may be seducing you today and perhaps you feel sad that you haven't the time to spare. A partner may desire more of your time than you'd like. If you can promise them your company this evening, you may both enjoy snuggling down and planning adventures together.

Thursday 14th

There may be an urgent job to do today which will need all your energy. This leaves you no time to wallow in your dreams and you may resent this. However, if you can combine your ability to see the detail in something, you may complete this job with satisfaction.

Friday 15th

Mars enters your relationship zone and brings passion and drive to the other planets already there. Partner time can be highly sensual, dreamy and active. Make the most of it. Building an environment based on what each of you value is important now. Keep talking and manifest the life you want.

Saturday 16th

Today's full moon can be a great equaliser for you. It can spotlight all that you hold dear and allow you to see if they still give you pleasure. Finances, your home and self-worth are featured now. Partnerships can thrive under this Moon if you share similar values.

Sunday 17th

Conversations may be fuelled with intense passion and wonder now. A lively exchange can take you back to your fantasy land with a lover. Messaging and short visits can be playful but seductive. Keep a level head and don't get caught in a trap unless you're enjoying the chase.

Monday 18th

Secrets, gossip and lies can all be rife today. The energy is sexy and intriguing. You may not need to push too far to learn something mysterious about someone. It could be spilled unintentionally over messages or emails. This can be harmless, but the espionage draws you in.

Tuesday 19th

You may be more outgoing now and stretching your muscles appeals to you. Family issues may need your attention as you could be seeking some kind of truth or justice. The world may seem too small or isolating and you may take your interests further afield. Play it safe and know your limits.

Wednesday 20th

Getting your own way, or at least asking for what you want doesn't go down too well now. You may have more luck sticking to the rules and getting on with your daily routine. A partner may be quite needy today and they may get disappointed by your lack of interest.

Thursday 21st

Today is a different story. You may return to your passions with fervour and bowl someone over. Travel and culture interest you more now and you may be more pro-active about booking something special. A lover may not understand your sudden change of mood, but it pleases them.

Friday 22nd

Be prepared for a passionate and love-filled day. Your creative and sexual energy is high, and you could be romancing your muse. Express yourself clearly and make your intentions known. There is powerful yet delightful planetary energy for you to access. Use it well and be productive with it.

Saturday 23rd

It's possible that you feel the change in you now. However, you may need to switch your attention to mundane jobs or something you voluntarily do for the collective. Your heart is wide open and attuned to where Mercury is guiding you. Pleasure, travel and finances may be the key.

Sunday 24th

You could be irritated today. This is a passing phase, so ride it out and refrain from causing any unnecessary upset. You may clash with an authority figure you see daily. Words can be powerful tools and you may be tempted to use yours this way. Think twice or walk away.

Monday 25th

Don't let your mouth run away with you this morning. You will need to abide by the rules and get things done despite wanting to discuss your dreams all day. A partner may help to bring you to a better mood later in the day. Talk about your shared future soothes you.

Tuesday 26th

Unstable energy can lead you to become restless and frustrated. You may wish to find a way of managing this. A calming walk in nature or practical activity such as gardening might help. Meditation can centre you and bring you peace. Lower your expectations of yourself and a lover.

Wednesday 27th

If it's possible to take a day off, do so. It may benefit you to drop into dreamland for the day and switch off from outside worries. Your inner compass is recalibrating and you should pay attention. Set your sights on new adventures and take the person you love most with you.

Thursday 28th

You may have a better idea of what needs to go from your life. It could be that your research has taken a turn and different things interest you now. This could be a sign of maturity or settling into a new way of creating, loving and expressing.

Friday 29th

Pluto turns retrograde today. You may go through a period of rearranging, discarding or completely transforming things concerning romance, creativity and how you learn. You may be keen for this to happen as it could be long overdue and you enjoy a good clear-out and decluttering session.

Saturday 30th

A new moon and solar eclipse open a window of wild card energy in your travel zone. As it also comes with blessings from Venus and Jupiter, you may wish to be impulsive in love or make a grand gesture. Be absolutely sure about this as eclipses can show our shadow sides.

MAY

. . . .

Sunday 1st

Your emotions may be a little unstable today. It's likely that you're feeling something shifting and not sure what it is. You might get a better idea of this by evening as it may concern travel or higher education. Perhaps you think that you're not getting enough of either.

Monday 2nd

Pull yourself back to your core values today. If you use your mind you may find a way of combining work with pleasure. You may have a curiosity for alternative options and need to explore these. Venus shifts signs and can bring you more need to discover beauty and secrets.

Tuesday 3rd

You may not be able to fix your focus on one thing now. A wavering mood can clash with your physical energy. Don't try too hard to be productive today as it may exhaust you. Instead, learn to go with the flow and whatever gets done is a bonus.

Wednesday 4th

You may have an overwhelming urge to create or be productive now. You might dislike being tied to one project at a time and may have many on the go. This may be a problem, so choose one and see it through to completion. Slowly and steadily works better for you.

Thursday 5th

It's possible that you feel like a volcano waiting to blow and need to get rid of this excess energy safely. Look for your soul group of friends and let off steam with them. They may be supportive and hold you in a safe place while you rant and rave.

Friday 6th

A soul search seems to have begun for you now and you may not understand why. Follow the leads you are given as you may discover things about yourself which go right back to childhood and no longer serve you. You may be inclined to do some family history.

Saturday 7th

Put your defences down as there's no need for them. You could be feeling more protective of your personal path and wish to not risk exposure. Those who love you are on your side and will understand your need for privacy. Listen to your inner cheerleader and find your voice.

Sunday 8th

Today you are more fired up and prepared to go deeper into your psyche for answers. This may be a solo journey but can be aided by those who have trodden this path before you. If you get agitated, know that you have the map somewhere inside of you, you only need look.

Monday 9th

Stubbornness will not win you any favours today. You may clash with a person in authority and be unwilling to listen to good advice. Remember that you must respect people's boundaries if you would like them to respect yours. Do your duties and retreat afterwards if you must.

Tuesday 10th

Mercury turns retrograde now and may cause you a few hiccups in the workplace and any long-distance communications. Travel may be affected, so get prepared by backing up devices and double-checking your travel plans. Make sure that all communications are as clear as possible to avoid misunderstandings.

Wednesday 11th

You may find that your search for inner truth deepens now. If you begin to feel overwhelmed, remember that you're better doing practical applications or putting things down on paper. You may be torn between wanting to act on your dreams and acting out of character by thinking outside the box.

Thursday 12th

It might be difficult to think straight today. You could be trying to balance your finances or getting things tidy and clean at home, but you could be getting nowhere fast. This may affect your self-worth and give you some doubts. Stick with it, this feeling will pass soon.

Friday 13th

Look at what you own and what you share with others today. It's possible that you can free up some finances by cancelling out of date subscriptions. It's also possible that the opposite is true, and you've forgotten a payment, and this will annoy you. A guiding light may appear now.

Saturday 14th

You may need to get to grips with changes in your creative and romantic endeavours. These will be minor, but you may see them as bigger than they are due to your keen eye for detail. Make sure that communications are completely clear of misunderstandings and avoid intense feelings.

Sunday 15th

Try not to react to difficult conversations now. It could be that you're the one who is blowing a fuse and making things worse. Retreat into your dream world if confrontation threatens to derail you. No one is budging from their opinions, so you would do best by leaving them to it.

Monday 16th

A full moon and lunar eclipse may reveal something in a conversation. This could be intense, so be prepared. Your energy may be reckless this afternoon and you could say one or two things which may cause trouble in the workplace. Make sure that you can back up what you say.

Tuesday 17th

You may be fuelled by a passion to discover the deeper mysteries of life. A sense of truth and justice may make you headstrong today, but using compassion and calm, you may get to the bottom of what it is you wish to know. This could enhance your family life.

Wednesday 18th

There may be heavy energy within your love relationship now. This can go two ways. It can be powered by passion and shared visions, or it can get volatile and you need to check in with your inner compass for direction. You could retreat and sulk about it.

Thursday 19th

Stay grounded today as much as you can. Get on with an art project or change something old into something more useful. You may not be feeling quite so romantic today, but you can still create a masterpiece even if just in the planning stage. Cooking a tasty meal could suffice.

Friday 20th

Today you have the inspiration and motivation to act wisely and follow a dream. You may need to go back to the rule book and envision it differently. Duty calls this afternoon and you may need to catch up with jobs or messages you've neglected recently.

Saturday 21st

Activity regarding your social life heats up now but can be chaotic whilst Mercury is retrograde. Watch that you aren't being scapegoated or made to do more than your fair share. Check in with your health today as your mental energy may give you physical symptoms. Listen out for important information that comes your way.

Sunday 22nd

You may experience some turbulence in relationships today. You could be lacking pieces to a puzzle or communication between you just isn't working. You may feel like throwing in the towel, but stop, pause and breathe. This is only a passing phase and a minor irritation.

Monday 23rd

Travel plans are sure to be upset today, so take extra caution. You may also want to be careful with what you eat as you could experience stress leading to indigestion. Don't be in a hurry to end a relationship now just because you aren't on the same page at the moment.

Tuesday 24th

Hold on tightly to your inner compass as all around you, things are happening which are beyond your control. Breathe deeply and try to let them wash over you. This will also pass, but you need to get a grip and stay grounded while it plays out.

Wednesday 25th

Mars enters your intimacy zone and can be probing, direct and assertive. If you wish to explore the depths of a relationship you can do so now, but be mindful that this energy can be argumentative too. You may have a lighter mood until evening when conversations get twisted up again.

Thursday 26th

Your emotions imply that you are more respectful of boundaries. You may have been put in your place and are now remorseful. This is a great lesson to learn. Humble yourself and apologise if necessary. It will be easier if you express regret and vow to respect that limits are there for a reason.

Friday 27th

You may be seduced into thinking you can transform a relationship simply by showing compassion and harmony. However, if something is going to end, it will do so whether you like it or not. Tread carefully today as timing is important. Accept that there are some things you can't change.

Saturday 28th

Volatile energy continues to upset you and could be the cause of misunderstood communications or travel plans going wrong. Venus now enters this zone and will bring more harmony and balance soon. You may be more attracted to simple pleasures or exotic cultures now, so save your pennies and indulge yourself.

Sunday 29th

Emotionally, you may be pushed and pulled today. You have the right energy and desire to search within your soul, but outside influences demand your time. This is a trying day where you may be tested. Have the strength to let something go or give up trying to hold it.

Monday 30th

A new moon puts you in a place of decision making. This is more likely to be at work or regarding your social status. You could be offered two paths, both of which will require dedicated time and study. Choose an incredible journey which will change much.

Tuesday 31st

Your mind may be busy processing new information and possibilities. You would be wise to keep it real and not wander into fantasy thinking. It's important that you take a responsible approach now as all eyes are on you. This can enhance your professional status whilst teaching you more about yourself.

JUNE
. . . .

Wednesday 1st

Lie low today as your energy may be depleted and you need to recharge. Good food and company can be nurturing. You may also wish to check out places you'd like to visit or other such things which can feed your soul. Friends can be a source of comfort today.

Thursday 2nd

Something regarding travel may have caught your interest and got you excited. This is nice energy and can feel childlike or adventurous. You could rediscover a pleasure from childhood and have fun being nostalgic. Home favourites delight you now and their simple pleasures can make you feel safe and protected.

Friday 3rd

Mercury turns direct now. You may find yourself going back over old ground and making some adjustments. This may involve returning to a disagreement or misunderstanding and clearing the air. With a nourished heart, you can turn to your inner compass and smile, knowing that you're fully aligned.

Saturday 4th

Introspection is favoured today. You may find that you're more able to look at old wounds and deep-seated fears objectively. There could be someone spurring you onwards with your inner work. Saturn turns retrograde now and will sort out your place in the wider world and where you feel obliged to others.

Sunday 5th

You have an enquiring mind today and may be fired up with questions. However, these are for your ears only as they concern your most private thoughts. If you're keen to understand your psyche better, look at your natural reactions, likes and dislikes. What is a habitual response or coping mechanism?

Monday 6th

The Moon in your sign makes you more centred and calmer. You could be doing admin or detailed paperwork now. Time-consuming practical application can be a good option for you. Make time to check in with your health and detox or declutter your body and space.

Tuesday 7th

Making an itinerary for a trip would be a good activity. There is great energy for exploring on paper and planning something pleasurable. This may distract from your work but can be done on the side or kept for another time. You may find it hard to decide on any one trip.

Wednesday 8th

Ground yourself with hard work or physical exercise today. You may be more productive now as you attend to things which can lift your spirits. Romance and creative projects may get a boost from your attention to detail. Aim for harmony and equality in the home this evening.

Thursday 9th

It may be difficult to concentrate today as your mood is centred around what you value most. This may clash with your wish to work on your personal journey. It may be that you're tired and your energy must be focused on your immediate environment with no time for exploration.

Friday 10th

Talk with a partner about expectations. You may each have different views that can be adjusted and improved. It's good to know where you stand and what others expect from you. This may involve a tricky conversation, but you'll be glad that you've cleared the air and can move on positively.

Saturday 11th

There is anticipation in the air, so prepare yourself for a few pleasant surprises. You may be completely in tune with a partner now and engage in activities which delight you both. Cultural dining can be a great way of satisfying your taste for the exotic. Indulge and enjoy yourself.

Sunday 12th

A seductive atmosphere may take your mind back to times past. There could be something which returns to remind you of its presence at one time. You may experience some regret or simply get a whimsical and nostalgic feeling. You may also decide that this has no place in your present reality.

Monday 13th

Your mood is more outgoing, and you may wish to continue exploring the depths of your own psyche. Family revelations may build a bigger picture or fill in missing pieces of a puzzle. Mercury, your ruler, enters your career zone and will help you negotiate and find answers.

Tuesday 14th

A full moon lights up your achievements within your family group over the last six months. There may be unfinished business surrounding this. You must remember that there are limits and boundaries which could be there to protect you. Don't push people who may not be ready to share.

Wednesday 15th

A blockage may present itself in your creative and romantic pursuits and you could be tempted to take this personally. Use this pause to reflect on where you are, where you're going and what you would like the desired outcome to be. You may not have access to all the facts.

Thursday 16th

A romantic overture may give you hope for a future trip to exotic lands. You may be impulsive and wish to stretch your boundaries to explore something new. This may spur you onwards to a new passion regarding travel and living a life with small luxuries. Start saving your pennies.

Friday 17th

See the world as it is and consider your part in it. Today you may feel that you can conquer anything you put your mind to. However, keep it real and aim for success in your immediate environment. This may mean that you make yourself available to others more than before.

Saturday 18th

You may have too many obligations today and could resent the amount of your free time this takes up. The only way to get through the day is by willingly getting all your jobs done. You may struggle to enjoy your evening as you could be tired and grumpy.

Sunday 19th

Shared dreams and a loving partner may help you relax more today. It's possible to connect to your floaty space and let yourself drift and switch off. You may not be able to fix or focus on anything in particular, so don't force it. Go with the flow of the day.

Monday 20th

Genius thinking early in the day may save you time and effort in the long run. You may need to do a last-minute rush to complete a job at work, but by evening you will feel good about it. Your inner compass reminds you that you're aligned.

Tuesday 21st

The summer solstice arrives with the longest day. You may be outgoing and optimistic as the longer daylight hours give you inspiration for the coming months. Your mind may be busy making plans regarding your career. Practical changes can be the source of joy, expansion and pleasure to come.

Wednesday 22nd

Try not to be pushy today. You may be putting all your effort into deep enquiries of mysteries beyond your knowledge. An emotional attachment to getting to the bottom of something or reaching a new height in your relationship fuels your passions and you may not stop until you've exhausted yourself.

Thursday 23rd

Get productive and let people in the workplace know how much you care. Venus has entered this zone and can bring love, harmony and money to your career. Go after what you want now, but do it with compassion and curiosity. Work may become a pleasurable activity now more than ever.

Friday 24th

Broaden your horizons today and you may exceed your expectations. You may be more radical than usual and find different ways of receiving pleasure. You could be dining out at a new restaurant or discovering a new culture which makes you want to learn more. Go where your fancy takes you.

Saturday 25th

Don't be put off by perceived limitations. They may be there as a guide and not a restriction. Learn to be flexible and adapt to new circumstances. If you try to push something it may come crumbling down and you could lose everything you've built so far.

Sunday 26th

Let your mind continue to flow with ideas and notions which thrill you. You may notice that your self-image is changing and you're more inclined to attract what you need in your life now. Explore your options and plan accordingly. Luck is on your side today and you may get a boost.

Monday 27th

Your head and heart are in sync, although you may have to filter or process some thoughts before you can believe that. You have a better idea of your own limitations and those placed upon you but can still motivate yourself to be assertive and driven towards your goals.

Tuesday 28th

Neptune turns retrograde today. As your inner compass, you may experience this time as vague or confusing. As it involves your close partnerships too, you must be sure to keep one foot on the ground and stay in touch with reality. Don't be seduced by illusions and unattainable dreams now.

Wednesday 29th

A new moon is a good time to think about your family and social circles. Consider your needs and wants and whether those closest to you provide you with them. What nurtures you? What feeds your soul? Surround yourself with loving and nourishing people you may consider to be your tribe.

Thursday 30th

Make sure you're protected today as you could be feeling vulnerable to attack. Alternatively, you may need to be with people who support and encourage you. It may be difficult to deal with changes in your romantic and creative endeavours as you worry about exposing too much of your heart.

JULY

....

Friday 1st

Showcase your talents and let yourself shine today. This is a favourable day for bringing out hidden skills and impressing those in charge. You may have broken through a personal barrier and feel more confident in your work. Let others bear witness to this and support your courage to speak out.

Saturday 2nd

Discussions with bosses or elders may be enlightening and give you a few new ideas to explore. If you feel stuck in any way, do a fact check with yourself. It may be that your daring to expose your potential has unnerved you and you're not sure where to go next.

Sunday 3rd

Your inner critic may be giving you some trouble now. It's possible that you've shrunk back into your safety net and decided to proceed with what you're more comfortable with. Wait until this mood passes and you will regain your self-worth. Practical work will distract you from worries.

Monday 4th

You may feel an urgency to complete a project or make a discovery. Be careful as you may be putting in effort that can exhaust you. It might be a good idea to strip down your obligations now and discard anything which can threaten to overwhelm you and make you ill.

Tuesday 5th

The energy shifts significantly today. You may be busy putting down roots regarding travel or higher education. Thrill-seeking may be a focus now and you have a burning desire to do more of what makes you tick. Be cautious as you may be prey to illusions right now.

Wednesday 6th

A conflict could arise today. This might involve finances and you may be thinking too big or spending on impulse. Have a talk with yourself. If it brings you long term happiness, then that's fine. If it's a quick fix you're after, think twice. Weigh it all up before acting.

Thursday 7th

Use your mental faculties today as you may need to justify your desires to push the boat out. It could be that you're being unrealistic. Get advice and refrain from following a whim. Check all the facts and look at all your options objectively. Aim for quality, not quantity.

Friday 8th

There is tricky energy this morning and your probing into minor details may uncover something distasteful. Be careful in conversations as there may be a tendency to speak without filtering your thoughts, and this could end in tears. Friends may be a source of comfort this evening.

Saturday 9th

Today you might have an underlying rumble which may intensify into an outburst of volcanic proportions. Your emotions are on the edge and you won't want to waste time dealing with petty squabbles. Something from the past may need to be discarded and toxic cords may need to be cut once and for all.

Sunday 10th

You may be in the mood for a cull. This could involve decluttering, transforming art projects or passing on things that no longer mean anything to you. Think big and expand your mind out to your future goals. Family members may help you stay rooted yet urge you to grow.

Monday 11th

Try to keep your long-term goals in sight today. You may be tempted to pursue other avenues of financial gain, but these will be short-lived. Acting rashly or out of character won't do you any favours and will come back to bite you at some point. Be wise and think of your future.

Tuesday 12th

You have the necessary energy to create something beautiful and intoxicating now. A project may excite you enough to spend a lot of your time and effort on it. This may be the start of something which can grow over time and produce satisfactory results.

Wednesday 13th

Today's full moon throws the spotlight on your creativity and romance. You may see a result or completion of the previous six months work. However, you may still be protective of this and not wish to make it public just yet. Be proud of what you have created and show it off when you're ready.

Thursday 14th

Check your health and well-being today. You may notice that you're doing too much for others, or for the greater good and not spending enough time on yourself. You may be stubbornly indulging in unhealthy habits in an effort to have something to call your own.

Friday 15th

Today it may feel as if something is at breaking point. Sit, be still and observe what is going on around you. The triggers you're feeling may be external and therefore have no power over you. Do the responsible thing and act within your personal boundaries. Stay safe and don't react.

Saturday 16th

Your ruler Mercury is on the heart of the Sun today and is receiving new downloads. You may experience this as a deeper understanding of what you need to feel loved, safe and nourished. Your intuition may be higher than usual now, so listen out for subtle messages.

Sunday 17th

There is excitement in the air, and it may be that you're floating on a cloud with a loving partner. Your shared dreams and visions may be elusive but nevertheless thrilling. Stay curious and think about how the two of you can merge energies and reach new levels together.

Monday 18th

You may be wearing your emotions like a badge today. You could be more open to empathy and can express your needs and desires easily. Make sure that you keep it real as your inner compass could be playing tricks with you. Share only as much as you feel safe to do so.

Tuesday 19th

You have a big heart today and others may be attracted to your optimism. On one level you may be searching for inner truth, on another, you could be extending your arms to encompass and nurture your friendship groups. Expect to find your quiet inner voice now.

Wednesday 20th

If you have an agenda today, you may wish to keep it quiet. This could be because you fear it being taken out of your control. You may like things the way they are and have no wish to change them. Allow yourself a few home pleasures such as favourite foods this evening.

Thursday 21st

You could be stubborn in the early hours as persistent thoughts fill your mind. Learn to differentiate your inner critic from your inner cheerleader. An emotional attachment to getting what you want may make you aggressive or stroppy. Allow yourself a small treat to satisfy a craving.

Friday 22nd

Today you may have a startling revelation which points towards your onwards path. This may clash with your mundane duties and you will need to recognise where the limits are. Remember that you must fact check everything now in case you are being seduced by illusions or false promises.

Saturday 23rd

Your psyche may be strengthened and parts of it healed as the sun enters this part of you. You may find that you have more courage and can speak up when you sense an injustice. You may also learn to say no and to take precious alone time for yourself. Make yourself heard now.

Sunday 24th

There may be choices presented to you today. These may be between work and play, but won't be problematic. It might be interesting to follow your thought processes and see where you end up. Ask a lot of questions and ensure that you have all the information you need.

Monday 25th

Friendship circles may suffer a disconnect today and need your input to put right. This may be difficult as you need to hear all sides of the story and may not be able to make a balanced opinion. If you're not directly involved, leave them to it and protect yourself.

Tuesday 26th

You have more compassion today and people may flock to you for support. You could be sharing and caring with a group who have been a source of comfort to you. This evening you must be careful not to speak out of turn. You may unintentionally upset someone.

Wednesday 27th

Your energy and activity are high today, and this is good news if you're planning a trip or need to study. You may like to reward yourself for hard work this evening and enjoy a pampering treat or your favourite food and company. A midweek date or get-together may satisfy you.

Thursday 28th

A new moon may be the green light you need to be brave and bold. If there's something you need to get off your chest, now is the time to do it. Jupiter turns retrograde and you may experience this as your search for life's mysteries taking a different turn.

Friday 29th

The planetary energy is challenging today. You may perceive that you're under attack or being wound up for some reason. This will pass soon, so ride it out. You may need to bite your tongue or lie low as the tendency under this influence is to be argumentative and blow a fuse.

Saturday 30th

Your head and heart are in talks and may give you a sleepless night. Dream messages may be disturbing or enlightening. If you can delegate your duties this weekend, you may benefit from time alone to work on things that are bothering you. This will include any health problems.

Sunday 31st

Today you may be navigating volatile energy. Old habits and conditioned behaviour may surface, and you may display childlike responses to limits or restrictions. Stay safe and keep away from anything or anyone who may trigger you and bring out the worst in you. Be responsible and mature.

AUGUST

Monday 1st

There is unstable energy in the air, but it can propel you into the future with a new vision. This may be a new cycle beginning in travel, pleasure and education. Ground yourself with practical application to anything you do today. A turning point or new perspective may have been reached.

Tuesday 2nd

Your social groups may offer food for thought today. You will need to weigh up what's in it for you, but it excites and tantalises your senses. Check your financial status before committing to a group project. You may be protecting or nurturing both yourself and the wider world.

Wednesday 3rd

The temptation to make a dream or new offer your new reality is overwhelming. However, you may need to take more time to consider this and talk to the people involved. Self-doubt may creep in, so you must discard this and look at the bigger picture. Can it fit into your life?

Thursday 4th

Your ruler jumps into your sign today. This is great news as he can help you organise your thoughts better. Conversations can be deep and intense now as you want to know the ins and outs of everything. Cover all bases and leave no fact unchecked. Do your homework thoroughly.

Friday 5th

Momentary struggles with your unconscious thoughts may be disturbing. You may have concluded that you need to make space for anything new to manifest. You might need to have a difficult conversation with someone or let something go which can be a little traumatic for you.

Saturday 6th

Be careful as you could be draining your emotional and physical strength. There may be some nastiness in the air around communicating or getting things started. Fear not, as other influences suggest that you have the right amount of compassion and empathy to avoid hurting someone unnecessarily. Family members may be supportive.

Sunday 7th

Try not to overstretch yourself today. You may be called upon for family duties which might irritate you. However, your close friends and interest groups share your dreams and visions and can give you the space you need to adjust any plans that can help you move on.

Monday 8th

You have a better sense of responsibility today and can blaze a trail for others to follow. You may experience a shift in your understanding of relationships. By evening, you could be more inclined to get back to any creative or romantic projects which need more time dedicated to them.

Tuesday 9th

Today may be challenging and you could see passive-aggressive behaviour or power games. These are likely to play out in your romance and social groups. You may wish to spend more time on one and the other is complaining. Don't go to any excesses when researching, keep it simple.

Wednesday 10th

Grab the opportunity today to control or change what you can. Earthy energy allows you to put down solid plans which feel aligned with your personal path. There may be one last piece of information you need to perfect this. Open your heart to good causes and the wider world.

Thursday 11th

You may feel like going the extra mile for others now, but be warned that this may lead to a regular commitment. A one-off is fine for now. Venus enters your most private zone and can add to your self-worth. You may feel fiercely proud or bold enough to speak your mind now.

Friday 12th

A full moon can highlight your mundane duties and the love you have for good causes. It may also bring health issues into focus. You may feel stuck and unmoving now, but this will quickly pass. Gear yourself up for a weekend of love and dreams with a partner or soul group.

Saturday 13th

You may have trouble organising your thoughts today as your emotions may be too tied up in ethereal and dream-like matters. Don't let this worry you, consider it as time off and a chance to disengage from the outside world for a short time. Partner time may be imaginative and romantic.

Sunday 14th

Sharing with your partner can refresh your sense of excitement and readiness for change and adventure. Your inner compass asks that you check in and ensure that you're still on track and under no illusions. Get ready to take the first step of demolishing the old and rebuilding the new.

Monday 15th

You could be starting the week all fired up and ready for action. Make sure that you have the physical energy to match. Try not to get ahead of yourself at this time, as the most important thing is that you take things slowly and have all the information.

Tuesday 16th

Great ideas may be flowing through you at great speed. You must put a filter in place and sort out what is truly realistic and what is a pipe dream. Keep an eye on your health now as you may be overdoing it and could suffer from burn out.

Wednesday 17th

Today you may be more grounded and ready to accept that some things will take their own time to manifest. This can be frustrating, and you could fall back into old habits or worries. Try not to listen to your inner critic. You are worthy of good things and now is your time.

Thursday 18th

You may have a boost of excitability and have difficulty staying still today. Set your mind on the steps you need to take and get them done before the energy changes and you realise you've missed something. Be your best self and organise, declutter and make room.

Friday 19th

Conflicted needs can cause you confusion today. What your heart wants and what your ego is saying may be two different things. Let this pass and breathe deeply. Use your practical skills to be methodical and distract yourself with hard work. Ignore your self-doubts or need for instant fixes right now.

Saturday 20th

You may have an extreme emotional attachment to moving, acting and implementing your plans today. Stay still and try to shift that energy to your mental plane. Thinking, communicating and researching may help to satisfy your need for urgency. Be inspired and curious. You could resort to childlike behaviour today.

Sunday 21st

You may wish to indulge in dreaming or switching off today, but you could be working overtime and have deadlines to meet. The key is to stay flexible as you may end up feeling like the weekend has gone and you had no relaxation time. Be guided by priorities.

Monday 22nd

It's possible that you experience a trigger today and can feel vulnerable. If you need to lie low or get support from like-minded friends, then do so. You might need reassurance of your role in the group or simply want to be with those who nourish and nurture you.

Tuesday 23rd

The Sun enters your sign. Happy Birthday! Use this month to be super-efficient, methodical and analytical. Look out for a surprise today, you may be treated to your favourite foods and company. Someone close may offer you a treat or reward. Indulge yourself and enjoy what is offered.

Wednesday 24th

Uranus turns retrograde today. You may experience this as volatile outbursts or abrupt changes of plans. Take this as a learning experience and ensure that your plans are infallible. However, listen to any suggestions to try something new as you may surprise yourself and accept that it has value for you.

Thursday 25th

Make the most of Mercury's last day in your sign. Mental activities such as research, planning, communicating or filtering are favoured. Your inner process may benefit from this and you may overcome certain obstacles that have been holding you back. Remember to have compassion for yourself if this becomes traumatic.

Friday 26th

You are likely to experience some frustration now as you can't have your own way. This may be as simple as a travel plan being rescheduled which doesn't suit you. Try not to argue with this, be accepting and flexible. The more open to slight changes you are, the easier they will be.

Saturday 27th

A new moon in your sign is the perfect opportunity to set goals and intentions around you. You can be selfish now and think about what you alone want. Other energy suggests that you may be stroppy or argumentative today, so think carefully about your new moon wishes.

Sunday 28th

A childlike manner will not help you today. It's possible
that you are sulky and when confronted with duties and
obligations you may have a tantrum. Learn to recognise what
triggers these feelings. If this is an old and outdated coping
mechanism, consider how you need to adjust it now.

Monday 29th

Your inner compass seems misaligned today. It's you who isn't
on board today as your mind is elsewhere. Perhaps you are
trying to justify recent actions and not getting anywhere. This
afternoon you may have a more mature approach and be sorry
for silly and unnecessary behaviour.

Tuesday 30th

A roadblock stops you in your tracks now. This gets you to
look at things objectively. Instead of going down a rabbit hole
with excessive self-study or learning about life's mysteries, ask
yourself why this attracts you. If it has meaning and adds quality
to your life, it will still be there when your mood changes.

Wednesday 31st

Aim for a balance of work and play today. You might have
duties to do which distract from romance or creative time and
this may irritate you. However, by evening you may be satisfied
with deep and meaningful conversations. Intense subjects may
entice you into midnight messages.

SEPTEMBER
·················

Thursday 1st

Go through your inboxes today. You may get satisfaction from deleting old messages and cancelling subscriptions you're no longer interested in. This will give your natural skills of decluttering and cleaning out a boost. You may come across something that tugs at the heartstrings, but you should leave it in the past.

Friday 2nd

You may experience some disturbances regarding communication and travel now. Find an ingenious solution and say no to any extra obligations. If you can change your perspective on matters of romance and be willing to accept a differing opinion your day may be easier.

Saturday 3rd

Your home environment could be your focus today. You may be assessing your property for the value it adds to your life. Finances may be an issue and you could find ways of improving these. A sale of your unwanted items might be good. Get rid of clutter and freshen up your home.

Sunday 4th

Self-love can be achieved by allowing yourself to say what you're thinking. You may need more courage to speak about a troubling issue. You can do this if you remember that everyone has personal boundaries which need to be respected. A partner may support you in looking at things differently.

Monday 5th

Venus enters your sign now. This influence can make you more desirable and compassionate. Be careful that you don't start offering your services to those who don't deserve them. You may have difficulty with a creative project or understanding where your limits are. Start at the beginning and work up.

Tuesday 6th

There is great energy today to get things done using your methodical mind. You may have a better idea of the route you need to take to achieve your goals. By evening, you could be tackling something in a completely new way, and you might even enjoy the challenge.

Wednesday 7th

Your mental faculties are strong today and you might wish to use them to research or trial something new. If you stay curious and determined, you may solve a long-standing problem. Think outside the box and you may not even have to push to get the information you require.

Thursday 8th

Today is a little more difficult as you may find yourself in a stalemate situation. Communications may be fraught, but you must exercise patience and understanding. Your best bet would be to take a mature approach and be respectful, honest and kind. You will be moving again soon.

Friday 9th

As the weekend approaches, so does Mercury retrograde. Prepare for this by backing up all devices, double-checking travel plans and avoiding signing any commitments. You might be craving alone time which could upset a partner. However, you may just have to do a lot of chores and have no free time.

Saturday 10th

Mercury turns retrograde as a full moon shines on your relationship zone. Be careful when romancing and aim for equality and compassion. Your inner compass grabs you and you may have a feeling that you're misaligned. Remember that you're adjusting a lot right now and you can recalibrate later.

Sunday 11th

If you are craving a day trip or mini-adventure, think twice. You are likely to run into trouble today and may find yourself stuck somewhere far from home. Satisfy your need by watching travel documentaries or making plans for another time when the energy is better. Communicate your feelings clearly now or stay silent.

Monday 12th

As the working week begins, you have sufficient energy to plough through your tasks with ease. This might be a mundane day but will be one you can look back on with some pride. It's possible to achieve all those things on your 'to-do' list with time to spare.

Tuesday 13th

Gather your favourite resources today and fill your cupboards with tasty meals to cook. You may be in the mood for little indulgences or eating for pleasure. Sharing these treats with a loved one can make it better. Thinking about travel opportunities or higher education may also be on your mind.

Wednesday 14th

This is a lovely day for setting your sights on your future goals. You may be able to put down deposits or make bookings which will give you something to look forward to. This can be exciting, but there may be some time to wait until a little venture happens.

Thursday 15th

If you put your mind to it, you can make positive changes today. A love relationship has a new focus and you may have cleared the decks for new growth to occur. Shared dreams might still be vague and unattainable at the moment, but you can hold onto them until you have more clarity.

Friday 16th

You might find it tricky to fix on one train of thought today. Ideas may flow through you but not stick around for you to grasp. If you experience a power struggle today, back away as you could get hurt. This might conflict with your core values and may need reassessing.

Saturday 17th

Self-doubt may creep back in now and you may experience aggressive behaviour towards you. Be the better person and stick to your personal boundaries. Don't be too ready to make peace until you get respect returned. Don't make excuses for someone else's actions or become a scapegoat.

Sunday 18th

Today there's a lot of challenging energy for you to manage. You should do your best to feel protected and safe. You may, be too vulnerable to deal with things maturely now. Hiding away for the day is your best option. Nurture yourself or find close friends who can support you.

Monday 19th

You may realise that a creative project is causing you more stress than happiness. This is a good day to look at the ways you express yourself and adjust or transform them. Your self-esteem may be growing, and you could come to realise that you've let something go on for too long.

Tuesday 20th

Change what you can and accept that you can't control everything. You may be realigning with your inner compass today and feeling good about it. This is good news as you have recognised that some things or people are just not meant for you and jar with your natural energy.

Wednesday 21st

If you're feeling noticeably confident and certain, you might speak your truth today to someone. Be warned that this may lead you on a deeply intense path and could rake up old wounds. Be sure that you're prepared for this. If not, hold on to your thoughts a little longer.

Thursday 22nd

The Sun spends its last day in your sign. You might have the right energy to declutter and make space for new growth. Unsettling feelings may niggle at you and you could be tempted to take a leap of faith. However, this may not go the way you wish.

Friday 23rd

Your ruler Mercury has nothing to say today. It's your job to listen for subtle messages and look out for signposts which may indicate a new cycle within bigger cycles. As he returns to your sign, you may be going over old ground or double-checking facts and information.

Saturday 24th

Don't be dismayed today if you feel that your dreams and
visions have disappeared. This may just be a pause for you
to check in with your body, health and daily duties. Earthy
planetary energy suggests that physical or practical activities
would serve you best now. Exercise and housework would
certainly suffice.

Sunday 25th

Today is most certainly a day to look after your own needs.
Get back to a creative project, connect with a lover or
reward yourself with a treat. The new moon asks that you set
intentions around equality in relationships, your self-esteem
and core values. Financial projects may get a boost.

Monday 26th

Keep within your limits now and continue to be good to
yourself. That little voice inside your head speaks directly to
you and tells you to schedule a time for something you love.
Don't worry about others today, make time for you and you
alone. Your dearest friends will understand.

Tuesday 27th

Turn your focus towards using your mental abilities this
morning. This may mean getting your tasks at work done or
putting in more effort to figure out a problem. If you persist
with a creative or romantic endeavour they may push back,
and you could lose your flow.

Wednesday 28th

Your health may be an issue today. This could bring up deep feelings and you may wish to discuss these with close family. Make a stand for yourself and dismiss anyone who undermines you. However, learn to recognise good advice when it's offered as this could benefit you in the long run.

Thursday 29th

Today could bring challenges that you'd rather not deal with. These could be financial, and you might need to set limits on your spending to afford a more comfortable life. You may factor this into the adjustments that your inner compass is making and resolve to look deeper into new possibilities.

Friday 30th

Your family of origin may need your help now. You could be called upon to settle a dispute or offer your experience with money and value. They may appreciate your knowledge and ability to discern fact from fiction. Be detective-like and root out the core of the problem.

OCTOBER

. . . .

Saturday 1st

Group efforts are essential today and may have some measure of success. Turn to your family and immediate environment for support in getting something off the ground. Today should be about your tribe or significant relationships. This won't leave much time for play which may upset you.

Sunday 2nd

Your ruler Mercury turns direct now and you could achieve more clarity and understanding of recent relationship problems. You may be challenged to do the right thing and could be inclined to excessive outbursts. Balance will be hard to come by until you've let the dust settle and had space from each other.

Monday 3rd

Conversations are easier today, but you might still need to tread carefully. It may be a case of returning to the beginning and retracing your steps with a different perspective. You would do well to think of this as a new journey with a new mindset which has evolved and matured.

Tuesday 4th

A good cause may catch your attention and you could be rushing headlong into a new passion without thinking of anything else. This might make you feel good and raise your self-esteem, but can also be a short-lived or misguided approach to something which isn't really meant for you.

Wednesday 5th

Try to sit still and observe yourself as an outsider. It may help to ground you and take in the bigger picture. You may be anxious or impatient if you can't do things your way. Use your methodical mind to analyse what is going on for you. Get all the information and filter it.

Thursday 6th

You could drop into a dreamy and floaty mood now. Partners may enjoy and encourage this. However, you must be sure to stay as realistic as possible as there's a risk that you avoid or neglect your daily duties. Be of service to each other with unconditional love and support.

Friday 7th

A sudden change of tactics could result in a romantic or creative project being scrapped or transformed into a masterpiece. You may have a continuous flow of ideas and wish to get practical today. Your instincts may tell you what needs to be improved on or discarded completely.

Saturday 8th

Enjoy connecting with your inner compass today, but be mindful that you could still be harbouring false hopes and delusions. You might need a reality check before making any commitment to new plans. By evening you may find that something is bigger than you and feels too overwhelming for you to tackle alone.

Sunday 9th

Pluto turns direct now and is done switching things up in your romantic and creative zone. A full moon may highlight your efforts of self-discovery over the last six months. Stay alert to what occurs today as you might have an important revelation about your personal work or artistic projects.

Monday 10th

Check your deadlines today as there could be something which has sneaked up on you and needs completing now. Be astute and check every tiny detail of important issues. You could be more driven today and have your sights set on reaching your goals in the shortest time.

Tuesday 11th

Treat yourself to something nice today. Schedule quality time for yourself with good food and company or simply an early night with your favourite TV show. You might be processing thoughts about finding a better home and work balance, and you may like to begin implementing that this evening.

Wednesday 12th

Your mood could conflict with your duties today. There may be a lot to do and you simply can't be bothered. You may prefer to stay in a state of bliss but have practical work to do. Take a mature approach and get all your chores done, then relax with a clear conscience.

Thursday 13th

Your productivity is higher now and you may be putting in more effort or making up for lost time. Use your mind and be discerning if you can. You could be learning something new or managing others and needing to use your negotiating skills. You could be involved in a dispute.

Friday 14th

Compassion and harmony are your goals now. It might be part of your job to maintain good relations with clients or seek out connections in the wider world. Find it within yourself to be a good listener and show empathy where it's needed. Be respectful and responsible with elders.

Saturday 15th

It's possible that something has touched your core and you have an emotional attachment to it. This might be something you've learned recently, and you could now decide to be more proactive about it. Friends and social groups provide the outlet you need to feel safe, nourished and loved.

Sunday 16th

Stay in your safety zone today and feed your soul. Maternal figures may be helpful, and you may wish to connect with family members. You might also return to childhood treats or have nostalgic conversations. There's no need to do anything much today except enjoy a day off.

Monday 17th

You could start to feel guilty and believe that you've wasted a weekend. Use this precious time to take care of your basic needs. However, you may also feel vulnerable or exposed and wish to be alone now. If romance or creativity isn't forthcoming, keep it for another day.

Tuesday 18th

There may be an issue which you have to confront today. Muster all your inner courage and speak only your truth. People may notice that you've found your voice and you could be attracting an audience. If this is unwanted, you may be able to express yourself another way.

Wednesday 19th

You could experience some challenges today which can set you back and upset you. Check in with yourself as these may be triggering old wounds or childish habits that no longer serve you. It's possible that you're reacting and not responding in an adult manner and this is causing tension.

Thursday 20th

Take a deep breath as there's better energy today and you may be more successful. You may find a balance between expressing your essential needs and being productive in the workplace. Someone may have heard your plea and has taken steps to make you feel more comfortable about being assertive.

Friday 21st

The Moon in your sign may help to bring you back to your centre and become calmer. You could be spending the day making a lot of connections or checking out details regarding travel and education. Allow yourself to tentatively plan a break or holiday. Making an itinerary will satisfy you.

Saturday 22nd

You may not feel like being with others today. Wrap yourself up in your studio or workspace and do what you do best. A little creative or personal research might excite and energise you. A good clear-out will bring out your natural ability to see what is taking up space.

Sunday 23rd

Saturn turns direct today and you may find that your mundane duties and obligations ease up now. Be prepared for intense love connections by emails and messages. Someone or something has piqued your interest and you may feel something you haven't experienced for a while. Investigate this exciting new opportunity.

Monday 24th

Your head and heart are in sync now and you might be following up on a lead which adds quality to your life. This could be a good cause, a community project or a role in which you can excel and be of service to others. Be sure not to take on too much.

Tuesday 25th

A new moon and solar eclipse give you a green light telling you to go ahead. Whatever has presented itself as a potential source of enjoyment has come at the right time for you. This may also be something mysterious and seductive which can meet your personal needs.

Wednesday 26th

Let go of what can never be and look towards the future now. Don't let things hang on to your energy and spoil your good mood. You may need to have harsh words with someone who refuses to back out of your life. Stay calm and be kind and respectful.

Thursday 27th

You have the right kind of energy to pursue a new dream today. It may be that you have newfound inspiration and are fired up to do something with it. Take your time as you should know by now that you are better when you have a plan and follow the steps.

Friday 28th

Jupiter returns to your relationship zone for a brief period. This may hint that you have unfinished business to deal with. A legal matter may come up to be reviewed. It may also be that you have a renewed optimism and faith with a relationship or important person.

Saturday 29th

Home and work duties may clash today, or you could be burning the candle at both ends and suffering for it. Mercury jumps into your communication zone and heats up the action currently going on there. However, remember that you must go slowly and take in all the information.

Sunday 30th

Mars turns retrograde now. This influence will help you to stop charging into new things. You may be more discerning and think twice before adding your energy to something which may potentially drain you. Today, however, you could be excitable and look forward to a clandestine meet-up with a mysterious person.

Monday 31st

You may have found your muse now and can put all your effort into making gold from lead. Your creative exploits may grow larger or become more profound. You could even be adding a taboo or occult aspect. Do be careful what you say to others as it could be frowned upon.

NOVEMBER

· · · · · · · · · · · · · · · ·

Tuesday 1st

Take everything with a pinch of salt today. The energy
suggests that you might become very frustrated or irritated
by little things. This is a passing mood and you would do
best to listen to the advice of your elders and not overstep
the mark in all areas.

Wednesday 2nd

Your mental abilities may be slow-going and confusing.
Remember that you must slow down now and skim things
back to manageable sizes. You may desire to switch off and
forget about things this evening. Unwinding with a partner
can help you to let go and relax. A love issue from the past
may return.

Thursday 3rd

Today you're more light-hearted and whimsical. Perhaps
you've drifted to your fantasy Island with a lover. Conversation
and romance flow easily and merge into one. Your wants and
needs are in sync. Enjoy this momentary pause of bliss before
the energy amps up again.

Friday 4th

Today you must keep one foot on the ground and try to stay
grounded. You could be at risk of wandering off and never
coming back. You can connect with your inner compass, but it
still holds elements that aren't real. Check in with your body
or do some practical activity.

Saturday 5th

Here is your chance to let go of karmic baggage you've been carrying around for a long time. You may have had a visit from the past recently, but you can now deal with it once and for all. Romance and creativity can be both exciting and annoying.

Sunday 6th

You might be inspired to do something great for the wider world. However, you may need to think smaller and realise your limitations. Conversations are karmic and you could be signing a deal which completes a legal or financial transaction. Don't attempt to control something you don't understand today.

Monday 7th

The energy may feel heavy for you today. There's a hint of espionage, secrecy and underhand dealings. Stay away from this and concentrate on personal pleasures. Put ideas for travel or higher education on a vision board and expand your horizons. This may be something you to do next year.

Tuesday 8th

A full moon and lunar eclipse close a window of wild card energy. This can entice you to spend more than you can afford and indulge more than you should. Listen out for subtle messages from your ruler who may divulge a secret or two. Prepare for an upgrade in your communications and contacts.

Wednesday 9th

Put your money where your mouth is or stay silent. You may be at risk of speaking out of turn or coming across as foolish. There is volatile energy around and you would be safer if you lie low and stay out of trouble. Don't overindulge on the good things in life.

Thursday 10th

You may be stubborn today and could clash with someone in authority. Your ability to read between the lines may expose a fake and cause some tension. Let yourself have a dreamy, floaty afternoon with loving or sexy messages to and from a lover. However, don't be taken in by falsities.

Friday 11th

It might be tricky to meet someone in the middle today. There may be a standoff and you could refuse to budge. This isn't going to move anytime soon, so look at things from a different angle. You will need to be humble and agree to compromise.

Saturday 12th

A weekend with your soul group could be calling you. It might be that your wider social circles have events going on that you're interested in. Alternatively, an evening with a lover can be emotional, sensitive, sharing and caring. Good food and company are the flavours of the weekend.

Sunday 13th

This is a lovely day for feeling safe, protected and nurtured. Friends and lovers could be involved, but so can maternal figures. You may wish to do things which remind you of your childhood. Stay grounded and don't let nostalgia get the better of you. Conversations with siblings can be uplifting and joyful.

Monday 14th

Whatever emotions you begin the week with can feel exaggerated today. You may notice that you feel happiness and sadness together which can be confusing. If you need time this afternoon to process this, be brave and express yourself somehow. Art or poetry might help you do this.

Tuesday 15th

Don't get carried away with secret messages to a lover. Although this may feel good you may need to get a reality check. The sooner you do this the better. You could be floating on cloud nine but need to get on with hard work and practical activities. Find a balance now.

Wednesday 16th

If there's something you need to say to someone, do it today because the energy is about to shift, and your focus will change. Take advantage of the Moon in your private zone to express intense and intimate feelings. A leap of faith is needed to share your deepest desires.

Thursday 17th

Family now becomes your main focus and there might be plans to be made. This is where you shine as a leader and you could be rallying the troops in preparation for celebrations. Try not to neglect your duties here as there may not be time to catch up later on.

Friday 18th

Take things slowly again today. You could be pushing against the flow in work, travel and your relationships. This can feel overwhelming and you may need a break to see to your own needs. Make it known that you will be available after you've seen to your own stuff.

Saturday 19th

Today you must aim for balance. Check your finances and look around your home. Is there anything which needs to be freshened up or given a new lease of life? Family members may pull together on a DIY project which brings more lightness, laughter and harmony your way.

Sunday 20th

Keep plugging at anything that you started yesterday. By evening you might have a better sense of who and what are your friends and allies. It may be a case of serving others while also having favours returned and this can make you feel good. Acknowledge that some people have different skills to you.

Monday 21st

You have another chance to express deep feelings to someone special. It might be that you've upgraded a relationship status and have moved on to a new level. This may feel strange if you decide to go public with it. Sweet words of love, encouragement and support are offered by family.

Tuesday 22nd

The emphasis is now on your family of origin and you may be leading the way or hosting parties. A nagging feeling of leaving something behind may bother you, but it is for your ultimate benefit if you can let it go with love. Grieve your loss if you need to.

Wednesday 23rd

Dreams and visions you've shared with another may be a topic of conversation today. Be careful because the energy suggests that you may be unrealistic again. Remember that your inner compass is still retrograde and is asking that you realign when you know exactly what you want.

Thursday 24th

A new moon in your family zone lets you set intentions for the next six months. There may be a big project which you can all be involved in. This may involve, truth-seeking, going the extra mile and broadening your horizons. Jupiter turns direct to emphasise this.

Friday 25th

You may feel extra tired today and look forward to the weekend. High energy may have drained your batteries recently and you may now need to unwind. However, there's still work to be done, just do it slowly and methodically with frequent breaks to recharge yourself.

Saturday 26th

You might enjoy a day of resting or doing something creative. This is also a nice day for catching up with people you haven't connected with for a while. Short and long-distance friends may appreciate you checking in on them. There may also be homework which needs completing soon. Meet your deadlines before the holidays.

Sunday 27th

Dedicate some time today to pursue things that you alone are interested in. These may involve making space for something new or putting down ideas for creative projects you have in mind. Take your time with these as they are seeds to plant another time.

Monday 28th

You are more outgoing today and willing to do overtime to complete your mundane duties. However, you may hit a roadblock, but this could be your personal energy that is flagging. Only do what you can and don't commit to anything more. Delegate your chores or politely refuse others if you need to.

Tuesday 29th

Look after yourself better today as you may still be exhausted. Give yourself some love and compassion or speak to family members who can help to relieve you of your obligations. You may find that an elder or boss is willing to give you a hand. Know your personal limits today.

Wednesday 30th

Partner time is highlighted as this may be your best way of unwinding and recharging. A lover may know exactly how to get you to stop doing so much and to let others do things for you. Phone calls and messages can wait another day because you could need to rest.

DECEMBER

. . . .

Thursday 1st

Listen to your intuition today and hold on to your inner compass. This might be a time of pause for you to realign and get things straight in your mind. Outside challenges can be ignored or put to one side whilst you recuperate and find your place again.

Friday 2nd

Your emotions may be larger than usual but can act as a catalyst for a big change deep within you. Introspection and truth-seeking can bring you some revelations about your inner workings and the mysteries of life which fascinate you. You could be putting some puzzle pieces together today.

Saturday 3rd

Be open-minded now. You might feel outgoing and more optimistic, but your energy may be lacking. Take this time to nurture yourself and gather your family around you. You may be inspired or likewise be the inspiration for someone following a similar path. It could be your turn to guide someone else.

Sunday 4th

Neptune turns direct now. All will become clearer very soon. You may have already had a glimpse of this. Don't push for answers, let them come to you naturally. Take a day off hard work and overthinking, and allow yourself some pleasure. Good food, company and travel documentaries may suffice.

Monday 5th

You might feel as if there is something you need to expand on now. This is possibly a relationship issue and you may need to open your mind just a little more. There is an air of irritation around you, but this could also be excitement and anticipation.

Tuesday 6th

Your family may need more attention today. Perhaps your wisdom is needed to negotiate or solve a small problem. Keep all lines of communication open and clear. You could be planning events which are in line with your dreams. Try to be flexible as you might be the one hosting or organising these.

Wednesday 7th

Be mindful of the energy today as it's deceptively peaceful. This may afford you time to research or make enquiries about projects you're passionate about. Your ruler is now in your creative and romantic zone and can amplify your need for knowledge of the right steps to be taken.

Thursday 8th

A full moon meets Mars today. It could illuminate where you're stuck or need to slow down. It may also highlight the completion of a work project which has been going on for some time. Congratulate yourself for this. You may receive a reward or bonus from a boss or authority figure.

Friday 9th

Friends and social groups might require your company this weekend. You may not wish to spend more time with them than you have to as you have other projects in mind. You could be dismissive of others and prefer to look after your own needs. Protect your energy today.

Saturday 10th

Both love and creativity may get a boost from Venus today. It's possible that you put a lot more of your soul desires into your art. You may also be realising that the way to success is to be good to yourself. Start by reading the rule book and following the steps.

Sunday 11th

Feelings of vulnerability may surface and trigger a few old wounds. These could be about your self-esteem and you may doubt your talents or romantic prospects. However, these are because of the shift within you and you would prefer not to expose your personal path to friends just yet.

Monday 12th

You may be conflicted today. On the one hand, you might want to tell the world what you intend to focus on now. On the other, you may be protective and defensive as a way to avoid any kind of criticism. Be brave and tell one or two close friends.

Tuesday 13th

Don't let anyone put you off or tell you that you aren't good enough. These may be your deep-seated fears and they could be triggered today. Own your part in the collective and stand up for what you believe in, including your human rights. Being witnessed is important to you.

Wednesday 14th

The Moon drops into your sign and you gain confidence.
Practical applications can show you that you are valued and
can give you a boost. You may begin planning how to woo
someone with your art and dedication. Beauty is in the detail
and you, more than most, understand this.

Thursday 15th

Heavy earthy energy can help you to stay grounded and
focused. You may find that time drags in the workplace,
but this acts as a bonus and you can get more done. Find
out everything you need to know about travel, learning and
connecting with others for the upcoming festive period.

Friday 16th

Don't be scared to take a leap of faith today. You might need
to jump right into something to fully understand it. This
immersive experience may give you the answers you require or
the impetus to investigate further. If it adds quality to your life,
then go ahead and leap.

Saturday 17th

You could be putting aside your personal projects and running
a long list of chores today. This will be fine if you take it
slowly and prioritise. You could get an unexpected surprise
from someone you may not have heard from in a while. Enjoy
catching up with them.

Sunday 18th

Try to find a balance between your mundane chores and your own agenda today. It may be difficult to find time for play, but you are doing the right things and joining in with groups to arrange, coordinate or plan a gathering. Stay mindful of any health issues today.

Monday 19th

The energy amps up to an intense level where communications need to be probing and precise. There may be many options for you to choose from or filter. It could be that you have deadlines to meet and you need to be razor-sharp with your attention to detail.

Tuesday 20th

Jupiter returns to your intimacy zone and you may be thinking about continuing your quest for inner knowledge. First, you must leave something behind. This could be that you delegate or discard a duty, but can also be that you adjust a dream and make it more attainable.

Wednesday 21st

The winter solstice brings you a day of reflection. The shortest day ushers in the darker nights and you must sit, pause and give gratitude for the year gone by. Think about the love that surrounds you and the inspirational people you include in your tribe. Your creative projects may become more profound in this season.

Thursday 22nd

The festive activities may be taking their toll on you and your energy could be lower than you'd like. It's important now to do what's important for the greater good and come back to your personal goals when you have a clear mind and more strength.

Friday 23rd

A new moon is the perfect opportunity to set your goals and intentions regarding art, expression and romance. You may have learned not to rush these things. Making a plan, a 'to-do' list or a schedule for the new year would be an excellent activity now. This will be beneficial in the long run.

Saturday 24th

Today you may be more loving and sociable. As the season dictates, you could be spending time with a loved one and sharing dreams and visions. You might be co-creating or having a pleasurable, cosy time together. Conversation and love flow easily and feel mature and responsible now.

Sunday 25th

Today it's important that you exercise self-control as you may be tempted to excesses which can lead to feeling unwell. Take it easy and be open to sharing and expressing love and happiness. You may find that others are attracted to the joy and optimism you show.

Monday 26th

If you feel tired, you must rest. If you feel irritable, then withdraw from potentially problematic situations. You might have overdone things yesterday and now need to pull back. You may be commended for being responsible and knowing your limits. Be an example to others in your tribe, especially the young ones.

Tuesday 27th

Indulge in special time with a partner and switch off from the outside world in your own way. It's okay to dream and drift to a fantasy island now. Enjoy a surreal time of love, co-creation and connection. You may feel more attuned spiritually today and give thanks for your blessings.

Wednesday 28th

If it's possible to continue relaxing and feeding your soul, then do so. You may get a boost from your inner compass and confirmation that your way is now clear. It might now be more obvious where you're meant to be heading for your personal growth in the coming year.

Thursday 29th

Mercury turns retrograde today and reminds you to keep your wits about you. You could be reviewing decisions made regarding love and expression and ensuring they are in alignment for you. Big gestures of love and soul-searching may need to be taken with a pinch of salt for now.

Friday 30th

You may be anxious to get on with things but still lack the energy. Listen to your body now and stay in a place of low activity. Your mind may also be doing overtime thinking up new schemes or plotting how the next year will pan out. Give it a rest today.

Saturday 31st

The energy today is heavy, and you may wish to decline any spontaneous invitations. However, you could just be stubborn and decide to bring your celebrations closer to home. Do what you love and enjoy your evening.

Virgo

....

PEOPLE WHO SHARE YOUR SIGN

PEOPLE WHO SHARE YOUR SIGN

. . . .

The valuable influence of warm and hard-working Virgoans can be felt in the smallest and largest of ways, from helping just one friend to serving the masses. From perfectionist performers such as Beyoncé to Nobel Peace Prize winners such as Mother Teresa, Virgoans have the capacity to guide and inspire. Discover the public figures who share your exact birthday and see if you can spot the similarities.

24th August

Rupert Grint (1988), Chad Michael Murray (1981), John Green (1977), Alex O'Loughlin (1976), Dave Chappelle (1973), Ava DuVernay (1972), Marlee Matlin (1965), Stephen Fry (1957), Vince McMahon (1945)

25th August

Blake Lively (1987), Rachel Bilson (1981), Alexander Skarsgård (1976), Ben Falcone (1973), Claudia Schiffer (1970), Billy Ray Cyrus (1961), Tim Burton (1958), Gene Simmons (1949), Sean Connery (1930), Faustina Kowalska (1905)

26th August

Keke Palmer (1993), Dylan O'Brien (1991), James Harden (1989), Evan Ross (1988), Macaulay Culkin (1980), Chris Pine (1980), Amanda Schull (1978), Melissa McCarthy (1970), Mother Teresa (1910)

27th August

Alexa Vega (1988), Patrick J. Adams (1981), Aaron Paul (1979), Suranne Jones (1978), Sarah Chalke (1976), Mark Webber (1976), Tom Ford (1961), Peter Stormare (1953), Paul Reubens (1952), Barbara Bach (1947), Lyndon B. Johnson, U.S. President (1908)

28th August

Armie Hammer (1986), Florence Welch (1986), LeAnn Rimes (1982), Jack Black (1969), Sheryl Sandberg (1969), Shania Twain (1965), David Fincher (1962), Jennifer Coolidge (1961)

29th August

Liam Payne (1993), Lea Michele (1986), Carla Gugino (1971), Lenny Henry (1958), Temple Grandin (1947), James Hunt (1947), Iris Apfel (1921), Ingrid Bergman (1915)

30th August

Trevor Jackson (1996), Bebe Rexha (1989), Johanna Braddy (1987), Cameron Diaz (1972), Michael Chiklis (1963), Warren Buffett (1930), Ernest Rutherford (1871)

31st August

Sara Ramirez (1975), Chris Tucker (1971), Queen Rania of Jordan (1970), Tsai Ing-wen, President of the Republic of China (1956), Marcia Clark (1953), Richard Gere (1949), Van Morrison (1945), Georg Jensen (1866)

1st September

Zendaya (1996), Daniel Sturridge (1989), Chanel West Coast (1988), Boyd Holbrook (1981), Gloria Estefan (1957), Dr Phil McGraw (1950), Barry Gibb (1946), Lily Tomlin (1939)

2nd September

Alexandre Pato (1989), Zedd (1989), Salma Hayek (1966), Lennox Lewis (1965), Keanu Reeves (1964), Eugenio Derbez (1961), Mark Harmon (1951), Robert Shapiro (1942)

3rd September

Kaia Gerber (2001), Dominic Thiem (1993), Shaun White (1986), Garrett Hedlund (1984), Fearne Cotton (1981), Redfoo (1975), Charlie Sheen (1965), Malcolm Gladwell (1963), Jaggi Vasudev (1957)

4th September

Yannick Carrasco (1993), James Bay (1990), Beyoncé (1981), Max Greenfield (1979), Wes Bentley (1978), Mark Ronson (1975), Damon Wayans (1960), Dr Drew Pinsky (1958)

5th September

Giovanni Pernice (1990), Kat Graham (1989), Annabelle Wallis (1984), Carice van Houten (1976), Rose McGowan (1973), Michael Keaton (1951), Freddie Mercury (1946), Raquel Welch (1940), Jesse James (1847)

6th September

Lauren Lapkus (1985), Pippa Middleton (1983), Kerry Katona (1980), Naomie Harris (1976), Idris Elba (1972), Anika Noni Rose (1972), Macy Gray (1967), Swoosie Kurtz (1944), Roger Waters (1943), Jane Addams (1860)

7th September

Evan Rachel Wood (1987), Oliver Hudson (1976), Shannon Elizabeth (1973), Leslie Jones (1967), Toby Jones (1966), Eazy-E (1964), Gloria Gaynor (1949), Buddy Holly (1936)

8th September

Cameron Dallas (1994), Joe Sugg (1991), Avicii (1989), Wiz Khalifa (1987), P!nk (1979), David Arquette (1971), Martin Freeman (1971), Bernie Sanders (1941), Antonín Dvořák (1841)

9th September

Luka Modrić (1985), Zoe Kazan (1983), Michelle Williams (1980), Michael Bublé (1975), Adam Sandler (1966), Hugh Grant (1960), Colonel Sanders (1890), Leo Tolstoy (1828)

10th September

Ryan Phillippe (1974), Guy Ritchie (1968), Jack Ma (1964), Colin Firth (1960), Joe Perry (1950), Bill O'Reilly (1949), Cynthia Lennon (1939), Mary Oliver (1935), Karl Lagerfeld (1933)

11th September

Kygo (1991), Tyler Hoechlin (1987), Ludacris (1977), Taraji P. Henson (1970), Harry Connick Jr. (1967), Moby (1965), Scott Patterson (1958)

12th September

Connor Franta (1992), Alfie Allen (1986), Emmy Rossum (1986), Jennifer Hudson (1981), Ben McKenzie (1979), Paul Walker (1973), Hans Zimmer (1957), Barry White (1944), Jesse Owens (1913)

13th September

Niall Horan (1993), Ben Savage (1980), Fabio Cannavaro (1973), Stella McCartney (1971), Tyler Perry (1969), Dave Mustaine (1961), Jacqueline Bisset (1944), Roald Dahl (1916)

14th September

Jessica Brown Findlay (1989), Amy Winehouse (1983), Ben Cohen (1978), Andrew Lincoln (1973), Nas (1973), Sam Neill (1947), Margaret Sanger (1879)

15th September

Jenna Marbles (1986), Prince Harry, Duke of Sussex (1984), Tom Hardy (1977), Jimmy Carr (1972), Queen Letizia of Spain (1972), Tommy Lee Jones (1946), Agatha Christie (1890), William Howard Taft, U.S. President (1857)

16th September

Nick Jonas (1992), Alexis Bledel (1981), Amy Poehler (1971), Marc Anthony (1968), Molly Shannon (1964), Mickey Rourke (1952), Peter Falk (1927), B.B. King (1925), Lauren Bacall (1924)

17th September

Melissa Hemsley (1985), Flo Rida (1979), Anastasia (1968), Cheryl Strayed (1968), Kyle Chandler (1965), Narendra Modi, Indian Prime Minister (1950), John Ritter (1948), Jim Rohn (1930), Hank Williams (1923), Billy the Kid (1859)

18th September

Patrick Schwarzenegger (1993), Ronaldo (1976), Jason Sudeikis (1975), Xzibit (1974), James Marsden (1973), Jada Pinkett Smith (1971), Aisha Tyler (1970), James Gandolfini (1961), John McAfee (1945)

19th September

Danielle Panabaker (1987), Lauren Goodger (1986), Skepta (1982), Jimmy Fallon (1974), Sanaa Lathan (1971), Lita Ford (1958), Twiggy (1949), Jeremy Irons (1948), Adam West (1928)

20th September

Phillip Phillips (1990), Jon Bernthal (1976), Victor Ponta, Romanian Prime Minister (1972), Michelle Visage (1968), Kristen Johnston (1967), George R. R. Martin (1948), Sophia Loren (1934), Anne Meara (1929), Upton Sinclair (1878)

21st September

Jason Derulo (1989), Maggie Grace (1983), Nicole Richie (1981), Liam Gallagher (1972), Alfonso Ribeiro (1971), Luke Wilson (1971), Faith Hill (1967), Abby Lee Miller (1966), Shinzō Abe, Japanese Prime Minister (1954), Bill Murray (1950), Stephen King (1947), Leonard Cohen (1934)

22nd September

Daniela Ospina (1992), Tom Felton (1987), Thiago Silva (1984), Billie Piper (1982), Sue Perkins (1969), Andrea Bocelli (1958), Joan Jett (1958), Nick Cave (1957), Rosamunde Pilcher (1924)

23rd September

Anthony Mackie (1978), Karl Pilkington (1972), Jason Alexander (1959), Bruce Springsteen (1949), Julio Iglesias (1943), Romy Schneider (1938), Ray Charles (1930), Mickey Rooney (1920)